# A PASSION FOR THE IMPOSSIBLE

*By the same author*

COME WIND, COME WEATHER
JOHN SUNG
URGENT HARVEST

# A PASSION
# FOR THE
# IMPOSSIBLE

## The China Inland Mission
## 1865–1965

by

LESLIE T. LYALL

HODDER AND STOUGHTON

"God loves with a great love the man whose heart is bursting with a passion for the impossible."

William Booth, founder of the Salvation Army

"I have found that there are three stages in every great work of God: first, it is impossible, then it is difficult, then it is done."

Hudson Taylor

Faith, mighty faith, the promise sees
    And looks to God alone;
Laughs at impossibilities
    And cries, "It shall be done!"

THE ELEVEN INLAND PROVINCES AND INNER MONGOLIA WITHOUT ANY WITNESS IN 1865.

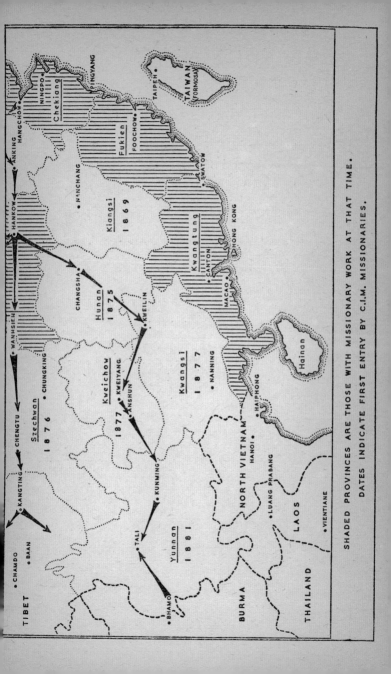

SHADED PROVINCES ARE THOSE WITH MISSIONARY WORK AT THAT TIME.
DATES INDICATE FIRST ENTRY BY C.I.M. MISSIONARIES.

# PREFACE

JUNE 25th, 1965 is the one hundredth birthday of the China Inland Mission. On that day James Hudson Taylor finally reached his epoch-making decision to form a society for the purpose of achieving the total evangelisation of China. Professor Kenneth S. Latourette of Yale University describes Taylor as "one of the greatest missionaries of all time and certainly one of the four or five most influential foreigners who came to China in the nineteenth century for any purpose, religious or secular".* What Livingstone did for Africa and Carey for India Hudson Taylor did for China. He and his followers opened up the mysterious and remote interior provinces of China to the Western world, complementing what the Jesuits and other Roman Catholic missionaries had previously achieved in this respect. They penetrated into the far west and into Tibet, into the wild mountains of the south-west where 150 tribes live and north-west into Chinese Turkestan and into Mongolia. In so doing Protestant work was initiated among all China's peoples and the foundation of the Christian Church well and truly laid. In due course other missionary societies shared the task of building up the Church but it was the privilege of the C.I.M. to plant the first flag in almost all the interior provinces of China. No other single organisation, Roman Catholic or Protestant, sent so many missionaries to China. The historic results for China itself of this Christian penetration cannot easily be estimated, but they were profound.

* *History of Christian Missions in China* by K. S. Latourette.

9

"The China Inland Mission was something unique in the entire history of the expansion of Christianity," said Latourette. Until 1865 missionary societies had almost all been associated directly with the historic denominations. From the very beginning this new mission was interdenominational and later it became international too. It has thus enjoyed 100 years of successful ecumenical co-operation. The Mission has had the backing of no denomination or powerful ecclesiastical body. In the early years Hudson Taylor was without many influential or wealthy friends. The members of the Mission declared their direct dependence for financial supplies on God alone. Later, other missions adopted a similar character and financial basis. Today, interdenominational missions are more widely dispersed in every Continent than denominational missions and their aggregate missionary membership probably exceeds that of all the older historic church missions together. Hudson Taylor thus set in motion something which has grown to vast dimensions and with far-reaching consequences for the world extending beyond his own Mission.

As a young man Hudson Taylor set out to test the reliability of the Christian claim that God is a living God whose recorded promises He is willing to implement. Again and again God granted Taylor convincing evidences that He did indeed respond to simple, straightforward faith. Taylor's faith grew with exercise and he based his whole life on a creed simply expressed in these terms: "There is a living God. He has spoken in His Word. He means what He says. And He is willing and able to perform what He has promised." Hudson Taylor has taken his place in history as outstandingly a man of daring faith, prepared to stake his all on God's promises.

William Booth, the founder of the Salvation Army, which also celebrates its centenary in 1965, once said, "God loves with a great love the man whose heart is bursting with a passion for the impossible". Hudson Taylor was such a man. His extraordinary accomplishments and the Mission which is his monument can only be explained in terms of the motto which is engraved over the entrance to the Mission's headquarters in north London: "Have faith in God". The centenary of the C.I.M. is therefore an appropriate occasion to bear witness to a sceptical world that there is a living God who is active in the world today and that He still responds to those who exercise a living faith in Him.

# CONTENTS

# HISTORICAL INTRODUCTION

CHINA's authentic history extends back for about 4,000 years. No other country in the world has such a long, uninterrupted national record. For centuries the religion of China was a form of polytheistic animism, including ancestor worship and magic, combined with a belief in a supreme Sky God, about whose nature Confucius refused to speculate. He used terms like *tien* (heaven), *shen* (spirits) and *Shang-ti* (Supreme Ruler) to express the early concepts of the supernatural. The simple, illiterate peasants were profoundly conscious of spirits and demons, while the emperor engaged in a dignified annual sacrifice to heaven at the Altar of Heaven.

Contemporary with the philosophers of Greece and Rome, there appeared in China a galaxy of philosophers no whit inferior: Laocius and Confucius in the sixth century before Christ and Mencius, Hsün-tzi and Mo-tzi in the fourth. Confucianism determined the social pattern of Chinese life. Later, entrance into the Civil Service was made dependant on examinations in the Confucian classics, and so determined the fact that China was a nation ruled by scholars and gentlemen rather than by economists, militarists or professional politicians. Taoism provided the mystical element in Chinese culture, adding the superstitious and metaphysical features of traditional Chinese thought and practice. But neither quite satisfied the spiritual aspirations of the Chinese. This need was met in Buddhism. Gautama Buddha was a contemporary of Confucius and lived in India, dying in 480 B.C. The religion he founded first reached China in 250 B.C. through Central Asia and via the Silk Route. But Buddhist missionaries were not formally invited to China until the reign of the Han Emperor Ming-ti in A.D. 58–76. Buddhism was immediately successful and, as one of the three religions of China, has continued to influence Chinese thought and philosophy deeply. From China, Buddhist and Confucianist thought and philosophy spread to Korea and Japan where they still exercise a powerful influence.

Christianity has made four major attempts to conquer China. This book concerns the fourth, but a summary of the first three will set the stage for the story. In the seventh century. Alopen, a Nestorian from Persia, and his companions were the first Christians to reach China. They were given an imperial welcome at the Tang dynasty capital of Sian in A.D. 635. The Emperor Tai Tsung gave orders for a church and a monastery to be built in the capital and initially there was some success. The Nestorian tablet, discovered in Sian in 1625, relates the coming of the first Christian pioneer missionaries to China. But this first twilight of the Christian religion was a false dawn. Persecution forced the Nestorians back into Central Asia. There Tamburlaine, the bloodiest and most cruel of all medieval conquerors, not only endeavoured to extinguish the Christian religion in Central Asia but his "Golden Horde", advancing through Poland and Hungary, threatened the very survival of Christianity in Europe. Pope Innocent IV was spurred to desperate action, and undertook the second Christian thrust into China.

In 1293 the Pope dispatched Friar John of Pian di Cartina, an early disciple of St. Francis of Assisi, to the Mongol Court in the centre of the Central Asian steppes. Although his reception was not very cordial he was the first European to bring back news to the West about the distant land of Cathay. He was also able to ascertain that the Nestorians had left behind in China the Old and New Testaments. Indeed the Nestorians had returned to Cathay proper from Central Asia in the wake of the Mongol invaders and when Marco Polo arrived at Peking, the Mongol capital, in 1375, he noted the existence of scattered groups of Nestorian converts. Marco Polo travelled to Peking at the invitation of Kublai Khan, although the two Dominican missionaries who set out with him turned back from Armenia! So the honour of becoming the first Roman Catholic missionary to set foot on Chinese soil proper was given to Friar John of Montecorvino in 1293, a Franciscan. He started a church in Peking and by 1305 there were 6,000 converts. But this promising beginning also ended in utter failure. Towards the end of the Mongol dynasty there was a severe persecution of Christians and the destruction of their all-too-conspicuous and foreign-looking churches. For the next one and a half centuries, Christianity in China was virtually forgotten. In the sixteenth century small parties of Franciscan friars, including Martin Ignacio de Loyola, made brave attempts to infiltrate into China from the Philippines where the Spaniards then ruled, but all were arrested, imprisoned and later deported.

The third effort to evangelise China was the most brilliant of all. It was made by the Society of Jesus, or the Jesuits, in the sixteenth century. Francis Xavier must rank as one of the greatest missionaries of all time, but he was unable to repeat his successes in India and Japan. China's doors were tightly shut to him. Matteo Ricci was therefore the first Jesuit missionary to succeed in gaining entry into China. He and his companion Valignani spent some time in Macao studying the Chinese language. From there Valignani, looking out over the water to China, once sighed, "Ah Rock, Rock, when wilt thou open, Rock!" At long last the Rock did open and Ricci was actually invited into China. At once he revealed his calibre as a missionary. He discarded his foreign habit and adopted the dress of the Chinese scholar. On arrival in Peking in 1601 he was extended imperial patronage and given a home of his own. Soon there were 300 converts in Peking itself and 2,000 others in the four neighbouring provinces. Ricci, with his exquisite tact and great reputation as a scholar, won respect for the Christian religion. He adopted a policy of synthesis in trying to make Christianity acceptable to the Chinese: he decided to his own satisfaction that the performance of the rites in honour of Confucius was not idolatrous and that the Chinese term *tien* or heaven was an appropriate term for God. His early death at the age of fifty-one was widely regretted. Between the death of Ricci and the end of the Ming dynasty was a very fruitful period for Christianity in China: it was characterised by intermittent persecutions and peaceful progress.

But the coming of the Dominicans in the seventeenth century introduced an element of controversy into the situation: they forbade any ceremony before the Confucian tablets and did not attempt, like Ricci, to adapt themselves to Chinese culture. The Jesuits were embarrassed and discomfited. As the Ming Court fled before the Manchus, the Emperor's mother was converted to Christianity and her son was named Constantine. But it was not granted to him as it was to his namesake to turn his nation to the Christian faith. However, by 1670 there were 100,000 Christians in eleven provinces of China with only twenty foreign missionaries. At the Court of Peking the scholarly priests were employed in manufacturing astronomical instruments and hydraulic devices. One of them at least was clear-sighted enough to see that the future of Christianity lay in the hands of Chinese clergy, while another wrote in 1701 of the character necessary in a true missionary to China:

"First, we need persons determined for the love of Jesus Christ to accept inconveniences of every kind, and determined to make themselves into new men, not only by a change of climate, of clothing and of food, but, more than all, in manners which are entirely opposed to the customs and character of the French nation . . . Men who allow themselves to be dominated by their moods are no use here; too quick a temper would do untold harm. The spirit of this country demands that one be master of one's passions and especially of a certain turbulent activity which wants to do everything and carry all before it by assault. . . ."

During the minority of the Emperor Kang Hsi there was a fierce persecution of Christians, and most of the foreign missionaries were imprisoned in Canton. But later this enlightened ruler came under the charm of the Jesuits because of their attitude to the Chinese people and their culture. He even wrote an inscription in praise of Christianity, using the term *tien* for God. But the rites controversy brought these promising beginnings to an end. Ricci, the Jesuit, had taken the opposite view from that of the Dominicans and the Franciscans, who regarded the Confucian rites as idolatrous. The matter was formally referred to the Holy See. In 1715 the Pope ruled against the Jesuits and decreed that all such rites by Christians and offerings on the graves of the dead must cease. He also forbad the use of the term *tien* for God, the penalty for disobedience being excommunication. (This decree condemning the Chinese rites and the Bull of 1742 were reversed in 1939!) Kang Hsi took the Papal decrees as a personal affront, and was furious. He ordered the banishment of all missionaries and the destruction of Christian churches. In 1722 the Emperor died and his successor Yung-cheng carried out the order, retaining only a few priests for his use at the Court in Peking. The Peking churches alone escaped destruction or desecration. Three years later fresh persecution broke out, the last foreign priest in China dying in 1787. This was the ruin of great hopes and the destruction of a flourishing Christian Church in China. The great Jesuit attempt to win China for Christ had, like its predecessors, failed.

Protestant bodies in Europe during the seventeenth and eighteenth centuries showed very little interest in spreading the faith beyond the bounds of their own countries and none at all in doing so in China. Dutch and English merchants in Far Eastern waters were far from being good advocates for the Christian religion. In 1637 the English made their first appearance in the Pearl River at Canton; their blundering refusal to observe the proper procedure made a very bad impression. But in 1807 Robert Morrison, the first Protestant missionary to China, reached Canton under the auspices of the London Missionary Society and was soon appointed Chinese translator of the East India Company. Morrison, because of the imperial edicts against Christianity, was compelled to restrict his missionary activities to the preparation of literature. In 1819 he completed the translation of the entire Bible. Morrison died in his early fifties and was buried in Macao in 1834. William Milne had joined Morrison in 1813 but, denied permission to reside in Macao or Canton, he and his mission colleagues made Malacca their base for reaching the Chinese. Milne's most famous convert was Liang Ah-fah.

But China was rudely awakened from her almost ageless sleep when, in 1839, the British Government decided to break through the barriers of China's isolation by force of arms. Hitherto scornful of foreigners and thinking of herself as the hub of the universe or "The Middle Kingdom", China was now forced into a war over the lucrative opium trade which England wanted to see legalised. A patriotic official in Canton ordered the burning of 20,000 cases of opium or "foreign smoke" worth nearly £4,000,000. This sparked off the first Opium War when British forces inflicted terrible suffering on the people of China and of Chinkiang in particular. Hopelessly outclassed by the superior technique of the "foreign devils", China admitted defeat in 1842 and signed the Treaty of Nanking on board the H.M.S. *Cornwallis*, which required the Chinese to open five ports to foreign trade: Shanghai, Ningpo, Foochow, Amoy and Canton; it also secured the cession of Hong Kong island, but not the legalisation of the opium trade. This final humiliation was imposed on the Chinese after a second war in 1858, in spite of American opposition. Between the two wars twenty or more Protestant societies, mostly from North America, established themselves in the Treaty Ports. But Elijah Bridgman and David Abel have the honour of being the first American missionaries to China; the American Board of Commissioners for Foreign Missions had appointed them in 1829 in response to an appeal from Morrison. Samuel Wells Williams, the scholar, and Peter Parker, the doctor, joined Bridgman in Canton in 1833 and 1834. In the 1830s the American Baptists sent missionaries to the Chinese and other societies followed suit. But there was little attempt to approach China unitedly and this error was to become a major obstacle to the progress of Christianity.

In 1800 not a single Protestant Christian lived in China, only Roman Catholics, scattered in isolated pockets, a down-trodden minority, perhaps a quarter of a million altogether. Even after fifty years and the Protestant occupation of the Treaty Ports there were only 350 converts compared with 330,000 Roman Catholics. In the deep interior it was left to the Lazarist missionaries M. M. Hue and Gabet, disguised as Chinese mandarins of the highest rank, to make their historic journey in 1844 from Peking through Inner Mongolia and north-west China to Lhasa, the Tibetan capital. There they almost succeeded in establishing a Roman Catholic mission, but when the Chinese authorities heard of them they were ordered out and reached Canton safely. This amazing piece of bravado, however, gave a completely false impression of the general situation in the interior. The Opium War had incensed popular feeling against all foreigners. Other Catholic priests were being hounded and hunted from place to place and Roman Catholic Christians were living under constant fear. In 1844 a supplementary treaty with China exacted guarantees that European missionaries should not be put to death!

Meanwhile, a powerful new pseudo-Christian movement was racking China, strange and abortive though it was. Hung Hsiu-ch'üan, when taking examinations in Canton, came into possession of the *Thousand Character Classic*, an exposition of the Christian faith by the first London Missionary Society convert in Malacca, Liang Ah Fah. In 1847, at the age of thirty-four, Hung came into direct touch with the Rev. Issachar Roberts of the American Baptist Board of Missions who gave him some instruction in the Christian faith. But Hung was a psychopathic case who had already had a mental breakdown accompanied by visions of greatness. He now began to teach the existence of God the Father and of Jesus the Son of God, the doctrines of Heaven and Hell and the Ten Commandments. But he also declared himself to be the heavenly Younger Brother of Christ and with some followers he founded The Society of the Worshippers of *Shang-ti* (God). Their main aim was a reign of "Great Peace" (*Taiping*). But as the movement was basically an uprising of land-hungry peasants one subsidiary objective was the public ownership of land.

The movement gained tremendous momentum and gathered large numbers of followers. In 1851 Hung assumed the imperial title, thus challenging the already hated and effete Manchu dynasty. Two years later, the year that Hudson Taylor first sailed for China, the "Taiping Rebels" won their most spectacular victories, capturing and burning Hankow, threatening Shanghai and making Nanking their capital. Hundreds of Roman Catholic Christians were massacred in Nanking, Yangchow, Chinkiang and elsewhere. In all the rebellion cost 20 million lives and eleven provinces were laid waste. A march on Peking failed and the Manchu Government, by calling in the help of the British, completely defeated the rebels. The leader of the British "Ever Victorious Army" was Lieutenant-Colonel Gordon, afterwards General Gordon of Khartoum. The Manchu Court saw in the Taiping Rebellion fresh evidence that the Christian religion was a danger to the empire and was prepared to resist any further Christian advances. One hundred years later the Chinese Communist regime celebrated the rebellion as the first major people's uprising against feudalism and imperialism. Hung Hsiu-ch'üan's pseudo-Christian movement might have succeeded in spreading Christianity throughout China, but for the fact that Hung was an unreliable and misguided fanatic. Its failure was both a national and a Christian tragedy.

## CHAPTER I

# VOYAGE INTO DANGER

1865. The summer season at Brighton was well under way. The hotels were filling up. London families were moving in. Nannies and children were making their daily pilgrimage to the beach. June 25th was a Sunday, warm and sunny. The sands were almost deserted. There were no bathers. The bathing machines were drawn up in discreet lines away from the water's edge. The beach donkeys were enjoying a Sabbath rest. All good people were in church. But pacing up and down on the fore-shore was a figure in black. He, too, had been in church that morning, but had slipped out during the service. For months he had been living in an agony of concern for the need of China—its material, but chiefly its spiritual, need. James Hudson Taylor—recently quali-fied as a doctor—could not forget the sights he had seen in China or the sorrows and the moral darkness of the Chinese people. The great majority of them had never heard the Good News about Jesus Christ. That morning in church the contrast between the congregation of rejoicing Christians and China's dying millions had proved too much for him.

For weeks he had known that God was calling him to undertake a major attempt to evangelise those un-reached millions. Yet his whole nature shrank from the responsibility. It was so unthinkable that he, an un-known young man, without any existing organisation behind him or any wealthy backers, should attempt anything so impossible. The strain of the inward conflict was so great that he had become physically ill. A friend invited him to Brighton to spend a short holiday, hoping that the sea air would do him good. But it was not the sea air which relaxed the strain. That Sunday morning Taylor surrendered to God and accepted his commission to lead a team of pioneers into the eleven inland provinces of China and Mongolia—at that date without any Protestant Christians or missionaries. An observer might have seen the lonely figure on the beach suddenly stop in his tracks, make for a seat and sit down. There he opened the Bible he was carrying and read the verse in Job xix. 23, "Oh that my words were now written! Oh that they were printed in a book!" Then at the top of the page he wrote, "Prayed for twenty-four willing, skilful labourers at Brighton, June 25th, 1865." The surrender to the Divine purpose was followed by a prayer in which Taylor irrevocably committed himself to this strange path of obedience. Writing of the event in later years Taylor said, "Out on the sands alone, in great spiritual agony, the Lord conquered my unbelief and I surrendered myself for service. I told Him that all the responsibility as to issues and consequences must rest with Him, that as His servant it was mine to obey and follow Him, His to direct and to care for and to guide me and those who labour with me."

Hudson Taylor's first assignment to China had been in 1853 when, at the age of twenty-one, he sailed from Liverpool to work under the Chinese Evangelisation Society. Seven years later and married he returned to England to recover his health. During his convalescence he completed his studies for the M.R.C.P. and translated the New Testament into the Ningpo dialect. But during the enforced years at home he lost none of the deep concern for the people of China. There were only ninety-one Protestant missionaries in China, mostly from North America, working with twenty societies. Their work was confined to twelve cities along the coast and Hankow, far up the River Yangtze. Taylor did his utmost to interest several British societies in the extended evangelisation of the Chinese, but in vain. All were too heavily committed and lacked the financial resources to undertake a task of such magnitude. April to June 1865 were months when the burden of China's need pressed heavily. Could nothing be done? Would no one see the millions dying without Christ and take up the burden too? How could the impossible be accomplished? What would God have him do? And so the crisis of June 25th was reached.

When Taylor returned to London the next day the strain had entirely gone and his wife hardly recognised him as the same man. On the Tuesday he paid a visit to the London and County Bank.

"I want to open an account," he said to the clerk.

"Certainly, sir. Your name, please!"

"It is not for me personally, but for the China Inland Mission."

This was the first appearance of this name, a name which defined quite simply the vast scope of the embryo Mission's proposed activities.

"And how much do you wish to deposit, sir?"

"Just £10, thank you."

The clerk may have seemed a little surprised, but he was not to know that this hitherto unheard-of organisation possessed no human resources at all as it faced a task of such dimensions. "Faith," as the late Dr. A. W. Tozer put it "is a redirecting of our sight . . . It is living through every circumstance of life with an Almighty God in focus to whom nothing is impossible."

In the following months Taylor received invitations to speak on China at conventions in Perth, Dublin and at the Mildmay Conference Centre in north London. In Ireland the '59 revival had prepared the hearts of Christian people for a challenge of this kind. His prayer for missionaries was gradually answered. Scores of people offered themselves in response to eloquent appeals on China's behalf. One by one men and women who seemed to have the necessary qualities were selected. The desirability of missionaries with good education was recognised but Taylor felt the need to be so great that he welcomed "persons of moderate ability and limited attainments" provided that they possessed the requisite character and spiritual experience.

Taylor now began to pray for a suitable ship to China and the money to pay for it. In April 1866 he was invited to give a lecture on China at Totteridge in

Hertfordshire. He accepted on condition that the advertising bills should announce that there would be no collection. Colonel Puget, the sponsor of the meeting, had never heard of such a stipulation, but he agreed to it. Taylor gave a stirring address on the Chinese people and their desperate need for the Gospel. The meeting was so deeply moved that Puget, the Chairman, whispered to Taylor urging him to change his mind about a collection, but in vain. So the meeting closed. The next morning, Puget, Taylor's host, was a little late for breakfast after a restless night. By the morning post Taylor had already received a letter, forwarded from home, from Messrs. Killick Martin & Co., shipping agents. They were offering him the entire passenger accommodation of the *Lammermuir*, a sailing vessel of 760 tons, with a request for £500 on account. Puget, knowing nothing of this, invited Taylor into his study after breakfast.

"You know, Mr. Taylor, that if there had been a collection last night, I was planning to contribute £5. As a matter of fact a few gifts were handed to me and here they are. But during the night God spoke to me. The desperate need of the people of China became so vivid that I decided to give you, not £5 but £500. I hope you will accept this cheque with my prayerful good wishes." Taylor needed no further confirmation from God that he should charter the *Lammermuir* and before long the full cost of the voyage was in hand.

Saturday May 26th, 1866 dawned bright and clear. The *Lammermuir* lay in the East India Dock, the Blue Peter fluttering from the masthead. She had a crew of thirty-four under the command of Captain Bell. The C.I.M. party were all on board. Sea-chests, camp-beds and simple furniture had already been loaded into the bare cabins, and the heavy freight stored below. The passengers said farewell to their relatives and well-wishers. Captain Bell gave the orders. The vessel cast off and glided slowly and silently out of the dock into the river. An easterly gale was blowing, so the ship was compelled to remain at anchor in the river all Sunday. But on that May Monday, a century ago, the *Lammermuir* sailed down the Thames, along the Channel and south into the Bay of Biscay on its voyage of destiny. Favourable trade winds carried her steadily towards the Cape. By the end of August the ship had crossed the Indian Ocean and was making her first call at the little port of Anjer in west Java on the Sunda Strait. The voyage had so far been uneventful except for the fact that twenty of the crew had professed conversion. But between Java and Shanghai they ran into two successive typhoons in the China Sea. Several time the ship almost foundered. The starboard bulwarks were swept away and let in water freely. Even the women had to help work the pumps. The jib-boom, the fore top-mast, the main top-mast and the mizzen-mast were all carried away. Heavy seas broke over the helpless craft and all hope seemed gone. Suddenly, even miraculously, the storm abated and the battered and crippled vessel managed to limp into the mouth of the River Yangtze. She was finally towed up the Whangpoo River to anchor off Shanghai on September 30th, four months after sailing from London. News of the arrival of the party and their preposterous intentions was greeted with scorn in the local Press. An English-language paper spoke of the missionaries as "madmen and lunatics" and asked "Why do not their people keep them at home in an asylum where they would be harmless to themselves and the community?" The old-timers prophesied that the venture was foredoomed to failure within a few months.

The beautiful and historic lakeside city of Hangchow was chosen by Taylor as the first base for the new mission. The seven original members of the Mission were already at work in Ningpo and three other cities of Chekiang. The Taiping Rebellion ended in 1865 after fourteen years, during which many provinces of China had been devastated and some of her finest cities reduced to shambles. One of these was Hangchow. The recent appearance there of American Baptist and Church Missionary Society missionaries had caused some rioting and angered the Roman Catholic missionaries. What would be the effect of the coming of this large party of foreigners? Before leaving Shanghai the young missionaries began to wear Chinese dress, the men shaving their heads and attaching queues to the inside of their Chinese skull-caps until their own hair should grow long enough! The 180-mile journey from Shanghai to Hangchow by house-boat took a month. The printing press, a large supply of medicines, and the equipment for opening a small dispensary accompanied the party. They quickly settled down to living in Chinese style, and to a routine of language study while Taylor set about preaching and medical work.

As soon as some of the party had learned sufficient Chinese, Taylor sent them out in pairs to three more cities. In the light of the recent wars, the humiliating treaties, and the opium trade it was not surprising that foreigners were greatly hated. Most Chinese were genuinely afraid and deeply suspicious of the "foreign devils" and their religion. But by moving about constantly among the people and by friendly approaches, the missionaries gradually disarmed the people's fears.

Less than a year after the arrival of the party in China tragedy struck. First Grace, the Taylors' eldest daughter of eight, contracted hydrocephalus and died after a brief illness. Then Sell, one of the seven original missionaries, died of black smallpox in Ningpo. The grief and shock to the young Mission were great. Matters were aggravated by disaffection within the ranks of the Mission. Some disputed the authority of the leader and called in question his methods. Only drastic disciplinary action saved the situation. But the work went on. George Stott began his apostolic work in the busy coastal city of Wenchow in 1867. Stott had persuaded Hudson Taylor to accept him in spite of his having a wooden leg. "The lame shall take the prey!" he quoted from Scripture to Hudson Taylor's satisfaction. The work developed into one of the most successful examples of church planting ever undertaken by the C.I.M. When in 1951 the missionaries withdrew from China there were two large and flourishing city churches in Wenchow and hundreds of country congregations as the result of the Mission's work, with a total of over 5,000 Christians in this one district alone.

In that same year, 1867, the work was extended into the neighbouring province of Kiangsu. Duncan, a tall Scot, made his way along the Grand Canal from Hangchow to Soochow and from there to Chinkiang, where the north and south sections of the Grand Canal join the River Yangtze. In September he travelled up river to Nanking, a city of 500,000 people. Only three years previously, 7,000 Taiping Rebels had been massacred in the capture of the city by the Manchu Government troops. Duncan could find no hospitality at any inn or home in the city. So he spent his nights in the ancient Drum Tower, the refuge of thieves and beggars, and preached the Gospel in the streets of the city by day. Generations later Nanking became the centre of extensive missionary work and had many fine mission institutions. A passing tribute to the pioneer who first penetrated the city for Christ is not out of place.

So far C.I.M. missionaries were working only in the coastal provinces. They were gaining experience prior to the planned advance into the eleven unoccupied inland provinces. In 1868, with this advance in view, Mr. and Mrs. Taylor moved their headquarters from Hangchow to Yangchow on the Grand Canal. This was the city where Marco Polo had, in the thirteenth century, been governor under the Mongol Emperor Kublai Khan. The wildest rumours about the "foreign devils" soon began to circulate: they ate babies, it was said, and used various parts of dead bodies for magical purposes. One Saturday a report went around that twenty-four children were missing. And at once an angry mob surged towards the mission house. Realising that the lives of the six missionaries and their children were in imminent danger, Taylor and Duncan (who happened to be on a visit to Yangchow from Nanking) made their way to the mandarin's *Yamen*. But they appealed in vain for protection. A mob of 10,000 rioted around the mission house until finally attempts were made to burn it down. The missionaries then had to risk breaking out from the house in order to claim asylum with a minor official. Some were seriously injured in the flight, but no one was killed.

Inevitably, news of the riot reached the British Consul in Shanghai. He welcomed it. For he was growing impatient with the frequent treaty violations by the Chinese in respect of British trade, and was waiting for an appropriate opportunity to bring pressure to bear on the Chinese authorities to put a stop to them. This was just the occasion he wanted. He immediately sailed up river to Nanking in the naval gun-boat *Rinaldo*. When the first negotiations with the Nanking authorities failed, Sir Rutherford Alcock, the British Ambassador, ordered a naval demonstration there. The Viceroy then reluctantly issued a proclamation reinstating the Mission and promising compensation for damages to property. The right of British subjects to enter China and to enjoy protection from the local authorities was also affirmed. The British officials in China were at first commended for their actions by the Conservative Government, but the new Liberal Government which took office that year under Gladstone changed the commendation to censure.

Locally things calmed down. In November Taylor was reinstated at Yangchow, an ideal centre for evangelising northward along the Grand Canal. But in England the storm was by no means over. A violent anti-missionary article appeared in *The Times*. During a debate in the House of Commons, Christian missions were both fiercely attacked and strongly defended. In the House of Lords the Duke of Somerset launched a particularly offensive attack on missions; Bishop Magee, in a brilliant maiden speech, made a crushing rejoinder, arguing that any Englishman had as much right to take Bibles to China as cotton—or opium! He also asserted the equal right under the treaties of missionaries to the same protection as merchants, neither more nor less. Thus the unheard-of party of nobodies who had sailed from the London docks unheralded such a short time ago were given sensational and certainly undesired publicity throughout the British Isles. The riot was headline news and the name of Hudson Taylor became almost as well known as the names of the new Cabinet ministers. But the incident was painful and embarrassing to him. Neither then nor at any time later did Hudson Taylor ever countenance any demand for compensation to the Mission for loss of life or property. Least of all did he ask for or welcome gun-boat protection. This could only do harm to the Christian cause. Yet there was nothing he could do about it. So while the debate continued at home, Taylor in Yangchow continued to pray and plan for the next stage in the advance.

## CHAPTER 2

# FAITH AS A GRAIN OF
# MUSTARD SEED

THE man who had called down such a storm of abuse
upon his own head was no mad fanatic or firebrand.
Never physically robust, he was during part of his adult
life an invalid or semi-invalid. His background was
humble. But soon after his conversion he made the
tremendous discovery that faith in God is a solid fact of
life; his life was transformed by that living faith which
links man's weakness with God's almighty power. Later
he became convinced that God wanted him to go to
China as a missionary. But first he felt that he must put
his faith to the test. He practised trusting God implicitly
in everything. He made a habit of praying to a Heavenly
Father whom he believed to be all-powerful and God
answered his prayers, if not always in the way expected.
In particular God met his need for money over and over
again in response to the prayer of faith. Why should such
practical business dealings with God be thought to be
any more visionary or idealistic than negotiating with
one's bank manager? Prayer is a practical person to
Person dealing with God: prayer of course includes worship, adoration and the acceptance of God's will, but if
the Old and New Testaments teach anything it is that
prayer includes asking and receiving as a child does of
its father.

Once, for example, when studying elementary medicine under a lecturer at the Hull School of Medicine,
Taylor was almost out of cash. The rent for his room was
due the next day. That night when visiting a destitute
Irish Roman Catholic family he gave them his last half-
crown, wondering whatever he would do for his rent and

for his food, yet content to trust God with an empty pocket. At breakfast the next morning the postman delivered an envelope containing nothing but a pair of gloves. He was mystified that there was no letter of explanation. But as he examined the gloves a gold half-sovereign dropped out! Taylor's joy knew no bounds. A cynic once suggested to Taylor that his must be a very hand-to-mouth kind of existence. "Yes," he admitted, "I suppose so. But it is God's hand to my mouth!"

Both Protestant and Catholic missionaries very naturally saw in the terms of the Treaty of Nanking a God-given opportunity to establish missionary work in the Treaty Ports. In 1853 Hudson Taylor reached China for the first time. He was not quite twenty-two. Shanghai was under siege from the Red Turbans, while the Taiping Rebels were at the height of their power. Prospects for extensive missionary work were very dim. There were by then only seventy Protestant missionaries in China altogether, with Americans outnumbering British by two to one. The London Missionary Society had the largest staff in Shanghai.

Early in his career young Taylor shocked the foreign community. One day he appeared in public in Chinese dress, his head shaven and wearing a long queue like any Chinese male under the Manchu dynasty. He thus sought to avoid the undesirable attention which his foreign clothes attracted as he travelled in the country districts and to enable him to live less conspicuously among the people. This outrageous behaviour brought Taylor almost total social ostracism. As he became more fluent in the Chinese language he extended his itinerations up and down the China coast. Sometimes he travelled with William Burns, the first English Presbyterian missionary to China who had figured prominently in a religious awakening in Scotland. Ningpo and Swatow were their chief places of call. The response in Ningpo was especially encouraging.

From 1855 the Great Powers and China were almost continuously at war. In 1857 the Chinese seized the Chinese crew of the *Arrow*, a small vessel flying the British flag, and Lord Palmerston's Government ordered the shelling of Canton, a defenceless city. There was terrible loss of life. The Treaty of Tientsin was signed in 1858, the year of the Indian Mutiny. But hostilities continued until the Chinese Army was destroyed and Peking occupied by Allied troops. In 1860, the Chinese signed the Convention of Peking which secured for European nations the right to establish embassies in Peking, added Tientsin to the other five ports, extended British sovereignty over Kowloon as well as Hong Kong and secured full liberty to practise the Christian religion in China. Liberty for Christians was thus secured at the point of the sword and maintained by threat of force, a fact which has never been forgotten by the Chinese people who have always deeply resented the "unequal treaties". Certainly these were agreements dictated by superior force. The Manchus regarded them as a national humiliation and hid their terms as far as possible from their subjects: even the mandarins were in all probability totally ignorant of them. As Christian missionaries were among the first to benefit from these events a very general belief became current that missionaries were the paid agents of foreign Governments. This persistent, ill-informed prejudice against missionaries has proved a major hindrance to the progress of Christianity in China. It is remarkable that it made any progress at all, for the iniquitous opium traffic, which brought immeasurable suffering to the Chinese people as a whole, was forced on China by a Christian nation. Thus the consequences of the first unhappy relations between China and the West were to make all foreigners appear in Chinese eyes as barbarous tyrants, eager to exploit the weak. This is the image of the foreigner which missionaries have tried—often in vain—to live down.

While the Second Opium War was in progress, Taylor was confined to Ningpo for three and a half years. There he met Miss Maria Dyer, the daughter of a London Missionary Society pioneer in the Straits Settlements. Her childhood was lived in an atmosphere of purposefulness to bring the Gospel to China. Her father worked with Robert Morrison and Robert Milne in Malacca in the production of the first Chinese Bible in 1824. He himself manufactured the first fount of metallic Chinese type ever made. He had always hoped to go to China himself to preach the Gospel. But this was not to be. It was his daughter who moved to Ningpo when the doors of China began to open. There in 1858 she met and married the "eccentric" independent missionary with the blue eyes and the fair hair, one as devoted as her father and herself to the cause of spreading the Gospel throughout China. Two years later, worn out with the running of the Ningpo hospital single-handed and in very poor health, Taylor returned with his wife to England.

Hudson Taylor's dramatic call to lead a daring advance into the vast interior of China came five years later. His faith was at first as a grain of mustard seed, but it was to grow until it became a huge spreading tree. Professor Latourette in *A History of the Expansion of Christianity* states that, "In no other land of so large an area and population was there ever a single society which planned so comprehensively to cover the whole and came so near to fulfilling its dream."

There have always been and still are—perhaps in increasing numbers—those who will challenge the right of Christians to preach their faith to people of other religious persuasions. One critic writes: "The fault lies largely with Christianity. It has the misfortune in every alien land of running counter to almost all cherished local institutions. It offends everyone. It antagonises every creed. It mingles with none, because its fundamentalist tenets deny the co-existence of any other faith or standard of morality." And Victor Purcell, in his book *The Boxer Rebellion*, says that "the Chinese attitude of mind makes it hard for them to believe that missionaries are merely concerned with instilling the idea into the Chinese that there is a choice of damnation or salvation". In other words, the Chinese have thought that the message of the missionaries is merely a blind to cover some other ulterior motives. There is of course truth in the first criticism, and there may be some truth in this interpretation of the Chinese mind. But a Christian is one who profoundly believes the truths of Divine revelation. He believes that there is only one God. To substitute another object of worship is the sin of idolatry. He believes that there is only one Saviour from sin—Jesus Christ who secured salvation for men through His death on the Cross. There is no way to God other than through Christ and no salvation in any other name. The Christian most certainly believes that all men are by nature lost to God until they are found of Him and that there is no hope in this life or the next apart from Jesus Christ. The Christian, therefore, believes himself to be under obligation to obey Christ's command to proclaim these truths throughout the world, since the present and eternal welfare of mankind depends upon his obedience. But it does not follow that he must do so clumsily and without an appreciation of and a respect for the beliefs of other men. Indeed, the Gospel must always be presented with courtesy and tact while preaching must be verified by example.

In drawing up the principles which were to govern his novel organisation, Taylor had the help of William Berger of East Grinstead, with whom he held long conferences to determine the pattern of this unique missionary society. The problems were discussed and the foundations of the C.I.M. firmly laid in the spacious and beautiful grounds of Saint Hill, Berger's home. A close friendship also existed between Hudson Taylor and George Muller of Bristol, the man of faith whose orphanages were such a remarkable testimony to God's unfailing faithfulness. The practices of the new mission were greatly influenced by Muller's wise advice.

"The China Inland Mission is totally unknown. We have no church or other ecclesiastical support behind us. So we are shut up to trusting in God alone for all our needs," Hudson Taylor might have said to Mr. Berger, as they sat on the lawn in the late summer of 1865.

"Should we not publicise our needs in some way? Surely people need to know in order to give?" Berger asked.

"No, I have never myself found this to be necessary. We must move men through God by prayer alone. And I mean by prayer *alone*: not by any form of solicitation or advertisement or by fund-raising schemes. I have proved this method to be one which God honours in my personal experience, and what He has done for me as an individual He can surely do for a group of people, however large!"

"I agree! But what happens if our income comes short of our needs? Won't that mean going into debt?"

"No! Going into debt is surely inconsistent with our basic principle of trusting God *alone*. Either we trust God alone or we adopt our own money-raising plans. We cannot have it both ways. To involve ourselves in expenditure for which we do not have the money is, to my mind, an act of distrust. If expenditure is in the purpose of God He must supply the money and He will. We can afford to wait until He does. I am sure that God's work done in God's way will never lack God's supplies."

"But let's be practical: how are the affairs of the Mission to be conducted?"

"Well, we will pray to God for funds. We will never spend beyond what God sends, that is what we actually have in hand or in the bank. On no condition will we allow expenditure to exceed income. This may mean times of straitness and even hardship for our fellow workers and apparent restriction of the work. But it seems to me to be the only consistent corollary of our interpretation of what trusting God alone means."

"But won't the Christian public get the idea that this is a rather hazardous method of running a society?"

"They may. But we believe that God will honour this method because it places all the responsibility on Him. At the same time we must make certain that our stewardship of the funds entrusted to us is business-like. There must be proper accounting and an annual audit. Everything must be just as business-like as in a commercial firm. We must show a sense of full responsibility to the Christian public and to the members of the Mission. Each member, however, must recognise that his faith is not in the Mission but in God alone. We on our part will faithfully administer all the funds committed to us."

"Don't you think that this may result in some inequality among the members of the Mission?"

"Not at all. We will work on the principle that all funds coming to the Mission, after all the essential overheads and working expenses have been met, will be equally shared among every member. The most senior member of the Mission will receive exactly the same as the most newly-arrived recruit. Of course, our allowance will obviously vary from quarter to quarter, but God will not allow His children to lack any good thing.

"And it follows that seeking first God's Kingdom, we must exercise absolute simplicity in everything."

This principle had already involved, for Taylor, living simply and in close contact with the Chinese people, even going so far as to conform with their cultural habits, dress and living conditions as far as possible. He was now to set the same standards before his followers. In organisation, too, Hudson Taylor believed in the greatest possible simplicity consonant with efficiency. The organisation of the Mission evolved spontaneously as the growth of the work demanded; the work was not in any way forced into a predetermined mould. Rudland, the young blacksmith who went to London to offer his services to Hudson Taylor in 1864, was impressed with what he found at the East London headquarters—reality, simplicity and intensity.

The decision that the headquarters of the Mission should be in China and not in England was one of great wisdom and of far-reaching importance. Nor was this initially determined by the international character of the Mission, which at first was solely British. Taylor never planned that it should be otherwise.

The founder would have been the last to claim that the principles and practices adopted by the C.I.M. were necessarily better or even more Biblical than those of other missions. They implied no criticism of the general practices of the older societies and Taylor was extremely concerned that support should not be diverted from them to the new channel. He tried to make this more difficult by refusing to authorise offerings when he himself or his colleagues were invited to the churches of the various denominations to speak. But while making no special claims for these practices Taylor firmly believed that the methods adopted were the God-given pattern for the C.I.M. God raised up Hudson Taylor and the C.I.M. to become monuments to one thing: the utter faithfulness of God and the practicability of a simple trust in God as a basis for living. One hundred years of stormy history have been a sufficient test of the validity of Hudson Taylor's faith. A total of more than 3,300 individuals have put these principles to the test and not found them to fail. Nor has there ever been any cause to modify the original principles or the practices in any way. God continues to honour a simple faith in Himself—even in the greatly altered circumstances of the twentieth century.

Burnaby, one of the Cambridge theologians, in the much publicised *Soundings* has written: "If God alters the course of events in answer to prayer, then the world will be unpredictable." But why should the world be predictable, except to a Determinist or a Communist? A sovereign Creator does alter the course of events in answer to prayer, as the story of the C.I.M. shows. C. S. Lewis called Mark xi. 24 "the most staggering promise": what we pray for with faith we shall receive. And he says that there is nothing naïve in this if we understand that it means what is within the compass of God's will and what is good for us. In this confidence the Mission was launched. In this faith the Mission completes its first 100 years.

## CHAPTER 3

# ADVANCE INTO THE UNKNOWN

HUDSON TAYLOR walked throughout his life "knee deep in miracle". He already knew God to be a living God, almighty and prayer-hearing, the God of the impossible. Naturally, therefore, he himself had a passion for the impossible. Humanly speaking, the task he had set for his mission was of this character. The whole interior of China was hostile to foreigners and virtually unkown. Yet with the vision and foresight of a Rhodes or a Raffles he planned not merely for a tentative approach to the partial evangelisation of an accessible part of China, but for the total evangelisation of every part. All his plans, far from being haphazard, were part of a well-thought-out campaign.

Immediately after the Yangchow affair in January 1869 he sent two men up river to Anking, the provincial capital of Anhwei. This was the first move into a hitherto unoccupied province. A riot followed in September and the men had to leave temporarily. But they returned. In December Cardwell joined Dr. Hart of the American Methodist Episcopal Mission in Kiangsi, the second of the eleven unevangelised provinces.

1870 was the darkest and hardest year in the Mission's history until 1900. Every step in the advance was fiercely contested. In England the undesirable publicity given to the Mission in the Press and in Parliament over the Yangchow riot had severely affected the Mission's income. Funds were consequently very low and faith was severely tested. Sickness was rife and there were several ill-afforded losses by death among the little band of C.I.M. missionaries. Those were the days before prophylactic medicines against cholera, typhoid, typhus, and malaria, all of which were a fearful scourge. In 1868, when hundreds of Roman Catholic converts were killed in Kweichow, French warships appeared off Nanking. Anti-foreign feeling ran high. In 1869 the massacre of twenty priests and nuns in Tientsin by a mob incensed at the building of a cathedral on the site of a temple caused widespread excitement. Feeling was so inflamed that Taylor had to order the temporary withdrawal of the women and children of the Mission in Nanking and Yangchow. The Chinese Government went so far as to circularise all foreign powers against missionary work. The circular was presented to both Houses of Parliament in England and some members actually pressed for the recall of all British missionaries from China. War again seemed imminent and threats against Chinese Christians persisted. Foreigners living in Shanghai scarcely dared sleep at night for fear of an attack.

Hudson Taylor himself suffered the most cruel losses in his own family. First his five-year-old son died. Then his wife contracted cholera just before giving birth to a son. Mother and infant both died soon after. Mrs. Taylor was only thirty-three. Overwhelmed with grief, how could Taylor continue his leadership? How encourage others to share such dangers and hardships?

In his personal sorrows and with the burden of leadership weighing heavily on him, Taylor was sustained by a fresh experience of God which revolutionised his whole life. He was enabled to appropriate in a new way the truth expressed by the Apostle Paul in the words, "It is no longer I that live, but Christ who liveth in me." He saw that by exchanging his own defeated life for Christ's, his own weakness for Christ's strength, he could live victoriously under any circumstances. Christ became to him more wonderfully real than ever before and his joy overflowed amid his grief. His fellow workers caught the infection of this experience and were inspired to new ventures of faith. Meanwhile the young churches were growing healthily, some even having a membership of over fifty. In Hangchow, a group of Chinese Christians actually formed a native missionary society and undertook the support of their own workers. They even published a magazine to keep the workers in touch with one another.

Hudson Taylor did not allow any trial to deflect his eyes from the goal. He was tireless in his devotion to his fellow workers. He travelled incessantly, visiting each station in turn, encouraging, exhorting, advising, preaching and caring for the health of all. He once made a journey of 500 miles to attend a sick colleague. This was in addition to the heavy administrative work for which he was solely responsible. (And there were no typewriters in those days!) No one was surprised when he suffered a breakdown. Delegating the leadership of the work to others, Taylor went home to England in the autumn to recover. It must have been satisfying to know that there had been more extensive itineraries in 1871 than ever before. In London he took the opportunity to form the first home Council of the Mission.

Eleven new stations were opened in 1873, including Shanghai. Cardwell, based on a Yangtze house-boat at Kiukiang, visited a total of 107 cities in Kiangsi, distributing the Scriptures. Henry Taylor travelled north from the Yangtze to the Yellow River to enter the province of Honan where the early Chinese emperors built their capital cities. The following year Hudson Taylor escorted Charles Judd to Wuchang in Hupeh and helped him to settle there. On the journey he had an accident when he fell down the companion-way, injuring his spine. At first he felt little pain. But when, accompanied by his second wife, he travelled home to England again on urgent Mission business, he arrived almost crippled by his injury and it was feared that he might never walk again. For six long months he lay prone on his back thinking and praying for the forty-three stations where thirty-five missionaries and sixty Chinese colleagues were at work. The future for him and therefore for the Mission was dark indeed. Things had seldom been so depressing. Little money was coming in. The Mission had few friends and no powerful voice or denomination to plead its cause. After the first enthusiastic support the Christian world seemed to have forgotten the C.I.M. There were no financial reserves. Could the Mission possibly survive?

At this moment of crisis its principles were put to an acid test, but "those feeble men and women held in their hands a lever able to move the world—its shaft their simple faith and prayer, its fulcrum the Unseen". Faith won through in daring fashion.

In the issue of *The Christian* for January 21st, 1875, there appeared "An Appeal for Prayer" by J. Hudson Taylor on behalf of more than 150 million Chinese. "There are nine provinces of China," read the article, "each as large as a European kingdom, averaging a population of 17 or 18 million each, but all destitute of the pure Gospel. About 100 Roman Catholic priests from Europe live in them but not one Protestant missionary. Much prayer has been offered on behalf of these nine provinces by some friends of the China Inland Mission; and during the past year nearly £4,000 has been contributed on condition that it be used in these provinces alone . . . Will each of your readers at once raise his heart to God and wait one minute in earnest prayer that God will raise up this year *eighteen suitable men* to devote themselves to this work . . . ?" This was the answer of faith to a desperate situation.

A month later, on February 21st, 1875, Mr. Augustus R. Margary, a British consular official, was murdered in Yunnan while on a journey from Hankow to Bhamo. China and Great Britain were again brought to the brink of war. No more inappropriate time could have been chosen, it seemed, for an appeal for more missionaries. Aware of this, Taylor wrote, "The difficulties are for human strength insuperable. Is not all Burma in turmoil? Has not Margary been murdered at Manwyne? Do not the latest tidings tell of Chinese troops massing in Yunnan? What again can our brother Henry Taylor and his Chinese evangelist do among the 25 million of Honan? We care not to answer that question, but we know what He who dwells in them and walks in them can do there." Taylor rose to the challenge of the impossible. In response to the appeal for eighteen men, sixty offered; nine of them sailed before the end of the year and one was accepted in Burma. Another eight followed in 1876. Some became outstanding missionaries.

In May 1876 the C.I.M. held its first annual meetings at the Mildmay Conference Hall in Islington. Hudson Taylor reported great progress during the first decade; fifty-two stations had been opened in five provinces, two of which had been pioneered by the C.I.M., and twenty-eight churches had been planted.

Completely recovered from his injury, Taylor set out for China again on September 7th, 1876, with eight new women workers. The prospects as he sailed were, politically speaking, very dark and many considered him quite foolhardy. This was before the days of wireless communications, and while at sea he was to be out of touch with world events until he reached Shanghai. Unknown to him until his arrival the Chefoo Convention was drawn up six days after the party sailed from England. This convention granted liberty for foreigners to reside in any part of China. Hudson Taylor took this event to be a direct confirmation of his step of faith. "Not too soon and not too late," he observed, "the long closed door opened of its own accord."

A part of Taylor's plan to reach the south-west of China was to establish a base in Burma. So Stevenson and Soltau were appointed to Bhamo. They arrived in October 1875 and after an audience with the King were granted permission to reside there. Their medical work rapidly gained a wide reputation among the Shan and the Kachin. The year following was one of tremendous activity when C.I.M. missionaries, taking full advantage of the newly-granted freedom, travelled a total of 13,000 miles. Baller and King travelling up the Han River from Hankow made the first entry into Shensi. Shansi, the "cradle of Chinese civilization", the north-western province of Kansu, and the huge western province of Szechwan above the spectacular Yangtze gorges were all visited in the same year. The only previous Protestant journey into Szechwan and Shensi had been made by Griffith John of the L.M.S. and James of the British & Foreign Bible Society in 1868.

In January 1877 Judd and Broumton commenced a journey by boat through Hunan into Kweichow. There, snow and ice on the higher mountains provided a cold

44

welcome. For the first time C.I.M. missionaries saw the aboriginal Miao (Meo). In the same month McCarthy, an Irishman, undertook what was said to be "foolish and impossible"—an east-west journey across China to Burma. He made the journey alone, travelling up the Yangtze and through the gorges into Szechwan where he opened the first station in Chungking. Then he turned south, stopping at Tali before crossing the Mekong and Salween River gorges and the high intervening ranges into Burma, a journey of 3,000 miles in seven months, preaching Christ all the way. After spending six months in Bhamo with Soltau and Adams, McCarthy went home to Great Britain to appeal for many new workers.

James Cameron, a Scot, was the greatest traveller of them all, the "Livingstone of China". His maiden journey took him up the Yangtze through the populous plains of Szechwan and into eastern Tibet, the first Protestant missionary to enter the country. At Tatsienlu he found a Catholic bishop! Thirty days out of Chengtu he reached Batang, where the French priest gave him hospitality. From there he went on to Litang, one of the highest cities in the world. To get there he was normally travelling at an altitude of 10,000 feet but the ten passes he had to cross varied from 14,000 to 17,000 feet above sea-level. The journey is one of the most arduous imaginable. Cameron then walked south for another two months until he reached Bhamo. Everywhere he sought to make Christ known. During his brief missionary career of six years Cameron travelled, mostly on foot, through all but one of the eighteen provinces of China as well as in Chinese Turkestan, Mongolia, Manchuria and the island of Hainan—an unparalleled feat. On his only furlough he studied medicine and qualified as a doctor.

All these intrepid pioneers found stoning an almost routine experience. They were relieved when there were no riots as there had been in Yangchow, Anking, and Ichang. All of them faced death repeatedly. They endured shame and rejection everywhere. They suffered incredible hardships. They had no settled residence and were continually on the move, proclaiming the Gospel. Judd was captured by pirates as he was returning from Kweichow through Szechwan. Later in the year Fishe died of fever in Kweichow.

In May 1876, Shanghai was the venue of an inter-mission conference of missionaries, an ecumenical gathering on the pattern of one recently held in Allahabad in India. Hudson Taylor was invited to read a paper. He was keenly aware of the widespread criticism that the long itinerations undertaken by the members of his mission were aimless wanderings and a waste of time and strength. So he chose as his subject "Itineration as an evangelistic agency". Uppermost in his mind was the fact that since the appeal for the eighteen all the nine provinces named in his appeal had been entered, the Scriptures distributed, and the Word of God proclaimed. The widespread journeys of C.I.M. missionaries were, Taylor argued in his paper, an essential preliminary to localised work; they were a prelude to a more thorough survey and the more concentrated work of establishing churches. He refused to discuss the relative merits of itinerant or localised work. To do so, he said, would be like discussing the relative merits of land and water, mountains and plains. Though he was under heavy criticism and misrepresentation he resolutely refused to enter into controversy. The fact is that Hudson Taylor from the first regarded local churches as the essential fruit of evangelism. His aim was the planting of such local churches everywhere. But they must be Chinese churches and not extensions of a foreign denomination. Their leaders must be Chinese and their church buildings of Chinese and not foreign design. Within the ensuing year Hudson Taylor appointed twelve missionaries and twenty Chinese workers permanently to the recently pioneered provinces, and forty converts were gathered. Faith was being vindicated. The initial goal was almost reached. Within ten years all eleven provinces in inland China had been visited by missionaries and the Gospel proclaimed. This in itself was no mean achievement. But the main task of evangelisation and church planting had barely begun. The general situation, moreover, was insecure, the door into inland China was little more than ajar and missionaries still faced the ever-present threat of deportation.

## CHAPTER 4

# FAITH REWARDED

THE spectre of famine has often stalked the land of China. 1877 marked the third year of one of the greatest disasters in the recorded history of mankind. From 9 to 13 million people died. The northern provinces of Honan and Shansi were the most seriously affected. Following up their initial brief visit to Shansi, Turner and James returned in the spring of 1877 to find the hills in the south a mass of spring beauty. But as they travelled north to Pingyang and Fenchow famine conditions became more and more terrible. Moreover, gaily-coloured fields of opium poppies betrayed the prevalence of this equally great scourge.

Famine relief was the first priority and, surmounting poor communications, four missions co-operated in this task. Dr. Timothy Richards, representing the English Baptist Mission, arrived in November. The widespread disaster affected over 30 million people. Hundreds of people died every day and were buried in open pits. There were cases of cannibalism, while the depredations of wolves from the mountains added to the horrors.

Mrs. Taylor had been living at home in England for some time for the sake of the children. After a separation of fifteen months Mr. Taylor joined the family in 1877. It was a wonderful reunion. But the famine situation in north China was weighing heavily on his mind. The welcomes were no sooner over than he said to his wife:

"My dear, I have a suggestion to make to you. Be prepared for a shock! I can't forget those dying millions in Shansi. I long to do something more for them. I obviously can't return just now. But what about you going?"

"Me! That's impossible! Who will care for the children? And haven't we been separated already for long enough? In any case what could a woman do? No women have ever been so far into the interior of China!"

Yet as they talked things over, Mrs. Taylor began to feel that perhaps after all it might be the will of God. Courage was not lacking—only that clear confirmation that it was what God wanted. And when this came, she prepared to go without delay. A special service was arranged to say good-bye, and when someone handed her a gift of £1,000 after the service, any remaining doubts were dispelled. "If you for Christ's sake can separate," said the accompanying letter, "I cannot give less than this, though the sum is ill spared from my business."

In Shanghai Mrs. Taylor was joined by two other ladies. With Fred Baller as escort the party made the long journey to Taiyuanfu arriving on October 23rd, 1878. This was the first time that missionary ladies had ever travelled so far from a Treaty Port into inland China. They at once threw themselves into the work of relief. In a speech at the Mansion House in London the Chinese Ambassador gratefully acknowledged their work. But the real significance of the experiment was the evidence it provided that there was no insuperable obstacle in the way of women, married or single, residing in inland China. The Mission leaders promptly appointed others to the city of Hanchung (Nancheng) in Shensi, where the work prospered to such an extent that an organised church resulted with a membership of thirty. Single women who ventured into the surrounding country everywhere found a warm-hearted reception. Others made the long journey to the remote north-west province of Kansu. The first party of women to make the two-month journey by house-boat up the Yangtze to Szechwan were shipwrecked in the rapids when their boat was holed on a rock. But they went on to begin work among the 10 million women of that province. Other women made the even longer journey to the extreme south-west of China. Mrs. George Clarke of Switzerland was the first foreign woman to enter Yunnan, where in 1881 she and her husband settled in the historic city of Tali, the most westerly point so far reached by Protestant missionaries. The town is set between majestic mountains and a beautiful lake, reminiscent of Switzerland itself. For two years they saw no other Europeans. When Mrs. Clarke died in childbirth the nearest doctor was six weeks' journey away. Thus in the course of five years women members of the C.I.M. had settled in six of the nine inland provinces, the first of any foreign women to do so. They were forerunners of many more who, facing loneliness and danger, would self-sacrificingly serve the women of China.

In 1879 Hudson Taylor returned to the field. Accepting an invitation to visit Holland *en route*, he addressed meetings at The Hague and Amsterdam; the first time that the needs of the Mission had been made known on the Continent.

Hudson Taylor was re-united with Mrs. Taylor in Shanghai after more than a year's separation. But he was so ill that the doctor ordered him to go north to the bracing seaside town of Chefoo, situated on the curve of a lovely bay. There his health rapidly improved. This was obviously a perfect place for a rest resort and ideal for a school for the children of missionaries.

Early in 1881, therefore, W. L. Ellison began to teach Charles Judd's two eldest boys. Up to that time there had been no school in China for European children. As the news of the opening of the Protestant Collegiate School spread, applications began to pour in from all parts of China for places in the school. The Chefoo School, as it was later renamed, became the best-known foreign school in the Far East. Not only did the children of C.I.M. missionaries receive an excellent education up to the age of eighteen but other missionary societies, diplomatic personnel and business people also patronised the school. In 1940 the Japanese interned the whole community and took possession of the buildings to form a military headquarters. The school never returned to Chefoo, but the name Chefoo continued to follow the school throughout its wanderings. The record of the school is a proud one: 20 per cent of the old boys and

girls have gone into Christian work and many of them
into the mission fields of the world; of these 168 returned
to work with the C.I.M. Others have made their mark
in many spheres: Kenneth Taylor, C.B.E., Canadian
Privy Councillor, Financial Advisor to the Canadian
Prime Minister and a Governor of the Bank of Canada;
the Hon. Allister Grossart, Canadian Senator; the Rt.
Rev. Kenneth Charles, Bishop of Ontario; the late
William Goforth, Professor of Economics at the McGill
University; Henry Luce, former editor of *Time, Life* and
*Fortune* magazines; Douglas Gonder, Vice-President,
Canadian National Railways; Carrington Goodrich,
Professor of Chinese at Colombia University; Thornton
Wilder, author, playwright and Nobel Prize Winner;
Richard Harris, Far Eastern correspondent of *The Times*;
Harold Judd, O.B.E., Controller of Salvage under the
Ministry of Supply in the Second World War; and a
long list of prominent scholars, doctors, lawyers, execu-
tives, architects and administrators. Some people have
imagined that the children of missionaries, through being
taken away from their parents at an early age, are under-
privileged and deprived in some way. The opposite is
usually the case, for God cares in a special way for the
children of those who have sacrificed all for His service.

In 1880 a young doctor and his wife spent several
months in Chefoo studying the language before travelling
on to Taiyuanfu, the Shansi capital. After leaving school
Dr. Harold Schofield of Rochdale first studied in London
University and obtained B.A. and B.Sc. degrees. He then
won an Exhibition at Lincoln College, Oxford, where he
gained a First Class Honours in Natural Sciences. Then
he won an Open Scholarship in Natural Sciences at St.
Bartholomew's Hospital, where he was awarded the
Foster Scholarship in Anatomy, the Junior and Senior
Scholarships, the Brackenbury Medical Scholarship, the
Laurence Scholarship and the Gold Medal. He was also
awarded the Radcliffe Travelling Fellowship of Natural
Sciences at Oxford and studied in Vienna and Prague.
During the Turko-Serbian war and the Russo-Turkish
war he was placed in charge of the Red Cross Hospital
at Belgrade. He then returned to England to become

house surgeon and house physician at St. Bartholomew's Hospital. He was known as one of the ablest young men in his profession, and a brilliant career was opening before him. When at the age of twenty-nine he declared his intention to become a missionary every attempt was made to dissuade him, but nothing could alter his determination to obey the call of God. The simplicity and the Biblical principles of the C.I.M. attracted him, and now as a member he had been commissioned to set up the first hospital in Shansi.

In his first year Dr. Schofield treated 1,527 out-patients and forty in-patients, performed forty operations and made 3,204 out-calls. In 1882 these figures were doubled. As 50 per cent of the male population were opium smokers, many of his patients were addicts. Not content with medical work alone, Schofield studied to improve his already good grasp of the language and delighted in the direct evangelism of street preaching. In 1883 he baptised the first four converts. Single-handed as he was, his mind often turned to the young men in the universities at home. He believed that the mission field desperately needed men of superior gifts, training and culture with good education and force of character. So he began to pray that some such might be sent to preach the Gospel in the crowded cities of China. It was as he prayed that God began to stir students' hearts in Cambridge, England. Two years later four of them were to come to this very city. But Dr. Schofield would no longer be there. After treating a patient Schofield himself contracted typhus, which proved fatal. Almost his last words were, "These three years have been by far the happiest of my life!" He was buried in a lonely grave outside the city. But his pioneer efforts were not in vain. Taiyuanfu was to become the centre of extensive Christian medical, educational and church work.

. . .

Since Margary's death, no one had attempted to travel near the Burma border. But in 1880 Stevenson and Soltau joined a caravan in Bhamo to make the first west-to-east crossing of China ever attempted—a journey of 1,900 miles. This journey emphasised the fact that China was really open to the Gospel and the desperate need for more workers. There were, it is true, already seventy C.I.M. stations in eleven provinces, but in 117 days the travellers passed through only two Mission centres. The total membership of the Mission was only 100—hopelessly insufficient for the task. Travel throughout China was becoming safer and easier as foreigners became better known. A British Consul reporting to Parliament in 1880 gave the credit for this state of affairs to the missionaries of the C.I.M.: ". . . they have managed to make friends everywhere . . . and have shown the true way of spreading Christianity in China."

The tremendous need impressed itself deeply on eight or nine missionaries meeting in Wuchang in November 1881. After a careful survey, they concluded that forty-two men and twenty-eight women were required immediately, and so pledged themselves to pray for seventy additional workers for the C.I.M. and large reinforcements for all the other societies working in China. No overflowing bank balance justified such a bold step. Far from it! But, hanging on the walls of the room where the group were meeting were the words: "For though the fig-tree shall not blossom, neither shall fruit be in the vine . . . and there shall be no herd in the stalls: yet I will rejoice in the Lord, I will joy in the God of my salvation." The Mission was young, small and poor. How could they dream of asking for so many reinforcements? Except from the standpoint of faith it did seem preposterous. The decision proved to be momentous and one which was to bring the Mission distinction and fame almost overnight.

The appeal for the Seventy appeared in the English publication of the Mission, *China's Millions*, in February 1883. Immediately God moved someone in England to give £3,000 on behalf of his whole family, and a supplementary £1,000 followed a little later. Nine new workers joined the Mission in 1882, eighteen in 1883 and forty-six more in 1884. The impossible was realised. The income, moreover, continued to keep pace with the increased number of workers. Dr. Andrew Bonar and Charles Spurgeon were among the Mission's warm supporters.

The evangelists, Moody and Sankey, were at this time conducting campaigns in Great Britain. Even the universities felt the impact of their preaching. A memorable eight-day mission was held at Cambridge in November 1882 and among those who were deeply influenced were the Cambridge cricket captain, C. T. Studd, the greatest amateur bowler in England, who was chosen to play for England against Australia on several occasions, Stanley Smith, stroke of the Cambridge boat and Montague Beauchamp, heir to the baronetcy and stroke of one of the trial eights. The appeal of the C.I.M. for the Seventy did not go unnoticed in university circles and now came to the attention of these young sportsmen. William Cassels and Arthur Polhill Turner, theological students at Ridley Hall, began to meet with their three sporting friends to share their missionary concern. Arthur's brother Cecil, an officer in the 2nd Dragoon Guards and his friend Dixon Hoste of the Royal Artillery linked up with the other five, and in the October term of 1884 announced that they were going to China as missionaries. So unusual and even startling an event captured both the headlines and the public imagination. The University was staggered. So was born the "Cambridge Band".

Remarkable farewell meetings were held at both Oxford and Cambridge. There were extraordinary manifestations of interest and sympathy throughout the whole country. Edinburgh University and its allied medical schools were shaken to their very depths and the wave of enthusiasm spread to all the Scottish universities. "The influence of such a band of men going to China as missionaries", wrote Dr. Eugene Stock of the Church Missionary Society, "was irresistible. No such event had occurred before, and no such event of the century had done so much to arouse the minds of Christian men to the tremendous claims of the mission field and the nobility of the missionary vocation. The gift of such a band to the China Inland Mission was a just reward to Mr. Hudson Taylor and his colleagues for the genuine unselfishness with which they had always pleaded the cause of China and the world and not only of their own particular organisation . . ."

The final farewell gathering at Exeter Hall in the Strand, London, on February 4, 1885 was without precedent. On a chill, wet night of pouring rain the building was filled to capacity long before the time to start the meeting. A delegation of forty undergraduates from Cambridge was on the platform. The issue of *China's Millions* containing the report of the meeting went into 50,000 copies. Never had a party of young men, so prominent in the sporting world and so distinguished socially, sailed at one time to be missionaries. Their welcome in China was equally enthusiastic and the meetings held in Shanghai, Tientsin and Peking aroused the entire missionary community. In Peking, where there were no C.I.M. missionaries, twenty-five members of several other societies signed an appeal for prayer which was sent to all missions in China. "If we would all unite have we not faith to believe that God would shake China with His power?"

Four of the seven men were appointed to work in the province of Shansi where there were just three mission stations and only fifty baptised Christians in the whole province. Pastor Hsi, the converted Confucian scholar and former opium addict was, however, beginning his apostolic work in the Pingyang district. He eventually opened forty-five opium refuges in five provinces and planted not a few churches as the fruit of his work.* The four men reached Taiyuanfu, where Dr. Schofield had served and prayed and died, in May 1883, the living answer to his prayers. Within eight months of the arrival of the Cambridge party four new stations were opened and a period of rapid and wonderful development began. The missionaries were greatly encouraged by a series of remarkable meetings in the capital at which Hudson Taylor and James Stevenson, as well as the four Cambridge recruits, took part.

In England the departure of the Cambridge Seven was commemorated in a book entitled *The Missionary*

* *Pastor Hsi* by Mrs. Howard Taylor (C.I.M.).

*Band, a Record of Consecration and an Appeal.* Fifteen thousand copies were rapidly sold, and a copy was graciously accepted by Her Majesty, Queen Victoria. An enlarged edition of the book under the title *The Evangelisation of the World* was sent by Sir George Williams to every Y.M.C.A. in the United Kingdom, and gave a great impetus to the missionary cause. Dr. Robert Speer, the missionary statesman, publicly stated that apart from the Bible this was one of the two books which had most influenced his career. The faith of Hudson Taylor was being richly rewarded.

"You must sometimes be tempted to be proud because of the wonderful way God has used you. I doubt if any man living has had greater honour," a leader of the Church of Scotland once said to Mr. Taylor.

"On the contrary," was the reply, "I often think that God must have been looking for someone small enough and weak enough for Him to use, and that He found me."

The subsequent history of the famous Seven was distinguished. Cassels became the first bishop of the west China diocese; Hoste succeeded Hudson Taylor as the General Director of the C.I.M.; Studd, after pioneering for some years in China, went to India and subsequently founded the Heart of Africa Mission, later to be known as the World-wide Evangelisation Crusade. The others served in China for many years with distinction. Sir Montague Beauchamp's son followed him and served as a medical missionary in C.I.M. hospitals until 1940. Stanley Smith's son became a missionary to Africa and co-founder of the Ruanda Medical Mission (C.M.S.).

## CHAPTER 5

# STRENGTHENED STAKES AND LENGTHENED CORDS

THE third decade of the history of the C.I.M. was one of consolidation after the rapid expansion of the first twenty years. The charm of the Mission has always been its simplicity. The early missionaries were just one large family and there was no official "red tape". Now the Mission had grown into a clan and needed rather more organisation.

In 1886 the field was divided into districts roughly according to denominations; there was an Anglican diocese, a Methodist area, a Presbyterian field and districts where Baptists predominated. Comity arrangements with other missions were reached. An advisory China Council consisting of the senior missionaries in each district met for the first time at Anking, capital of Anhwei Province. James Stevenson was appointed Deputy China Director. In England a new headquarters and training centre were set up at Newington Green in Islington, and the administration there was further strengthened.

But interest in the spectacular work now developing in China was no longer confined to Great Britain. Until June 1865 Hudson Taylor was totally unknown outside a small circle in Great Britain. America was preoccupied with the Civil War which ended that very year and was suffering from the shock of the assassination of their President, Abraham Lincoln. But twenty years later the news of Hudson Taylor's pioneer work in China had reached the United States. At the invitation of Henry W. Frost of Princeton University and D. L. Moody, Hudson Taylor visited the United States in 1888 to speak at the Northfield Conference and at a conference for Bible study at Niagara. When Taylor arrived he had no plans at all to extend the work beyond Great Britain, yet twelve weeks later, to his own amazement, he found himself sailing for China with fourteen American recruits, whose support was fully provided. This development was totally unexpected and unplanned, and severely criticised in England. But the London Council eventually agreed that the hand of the Lord was in this: it was not a device of man.

In the ensuing year Taylor accepted invitations to Sweden and Norway. In Sweden he was received by Queen Sophia in private audience. There was interest, too, in Germany and Finland. Eventually councils were set up in all these countries and in Australia, which now began to send missionaries to China. Henry Frost was appointed the first Home Director in North America. In this way and almost against Hudson Taylor's own judgement the Mission became international in character as it was already interdenominational.

Thirty different countries were eventually represented in the Mission, either as full members or as associates. Seventy years have amply demonstrated the feasibility of international co-operation. Today, different nationalities work together on the same station; doctors, trained in different techniques, work in the same hospitals and the funds from all countries are pooled, each member of the Mission receiving an exactly equal share. The international character of the Mission has also stood the severe strain of two world wars. And between members of different denominations, there is complete mutual respect and confidence. In spite of many superficial differences there is a deep spiritual unity.

The recent publicity given to the Mission by the Cambridge Seven did not go to Hudson Taylor's head. Nor did it incline him to rest on his oars. He was, at sixty years of age, still full of faith and the spirit of venture. The first meeting of the China Council in December 1886 agreed to cable home the following message, "Banded prayer next year 100 new workers send soon as possible". As with previous appeals this fresh leap of faith was not based on an increased income, nor was it faith gone mad. At least 100 new workers were clearly needed if the advances already made were to be consolidated and strong churches established. The impossible happened. The prayer for the Hundred was fully answered by the end of 1887 when all were either in China or on their way there. Six hundred in all offered: 102 were selected. To match the increase in personnel there was a corresponding rise in income that year from £22,000 to £33,700. Ten thousand pounds of this total came in eleven gifts, so involving little extra office work. But no less valuable were the small gifts of the poor. One lady wrote that "she could do without meat but the heathen could not do without the Gospel". The publication of this letter inspired five men to give £500 each. The first of them said, "All I have ever given to God's work has not cost me a mutton chop!" During the six years following 1880 the Mission almost doubled its membership. Now it was increased by 100 more, in spite of having no guaranteed income nor any influential committee to underwrite it if necessary.

In 1887, Queen Victoria celebrated her Jubilee and the Mission its coming of age. When the Queen had come to the throne in 1837, China was a sealed land: Protestant missionaries were confined to Canton, where they had been barely tolerated under the protection of the East India Company. Fifty years later the whole of China was open to the Gospel.

The Hundred were quickly dispersed throughout the country and gave a tremendous impetus to the work. Floods and famine wrought repeated disasters among the people. Death removed key Mission personnel who could ill be afforded, but nothing could deter Hudson Taylor. In 1889 he visited England again. While staying at Hastings he wrote a remarkable paper entitled "To Every Creature". This outlined a plan for realising the passion of his life—the total evangelisation of China. The paper was prepared for the 1890 Missionary Conference in Shanghai, when 400 delegates from forty societies representing every province in China met. Hudson Taylor preached the opening sermon and challenged the assembly with the necessity to preach the Gospel in every district, town, village and hamlet of China and that soon. He maintained that the current total of only 40,000 Protestant converts in the whole of China was far too small. (There were 500,000 Roman Catholics). He proceeded to commend the suggestion to send out an appeal to the home countries for 1,000 additional evangelists—all men! The Conference adopted the suggestion and addressed a united appeal for 1,000 men to all the Protestant churches of Christian lands. The Conference also agreed to produce a new Union Version of the Scriptures to supercede all previous translations. Fred Baller of the C.I.M., who had already produced a primer widely used in the consular and customs' services and other scholarly works, became an eminent member of the Union Bible Committee of Translators. In 1900 his analytical Chinese-English dictionary was published. This was the basis for a standard dictionary by R. A. Mathews of the C.I.M. Belatedly Mathews received a D.Litt. from Melbourne University for his scholarly work.

The appeal for the Thousand met with an enthusiastic response from European countries where the churches were in the midst of spiritual revival. Every mission in China experienced an access of new missionaries but the C.I.M. in particular benefited. On February 17th, 1891, the largest party ever to disembark at Shanghai at one time arrived from North America— thirty-five men and women of Scandinavian descent. Fifteen more arrived later. Providentially, a new and greatly-enlarged headquarters building which had just replaced the old rented premises made it possible to receive this large number of reinforcements. These premises in the Hongkew district were the timely gift of Archibald Orr Ewing, a British businessman, who also gave up his business to become a missionary to China himself. This munificent gift was, like the loaves in the hand of Christ, to be multiplied many times over in future years.

The whole Christian world was stirred by Hudson Taylor's leaflet. In 1892 the now well-known missionary pioneer was invited to speak at the Keswick Convention in England. He had become a world figure. Reinforcements began to arrive from Australasia and from the continent of Europe, as well as from North America. In the five months between October 1890 and March 1891 no less than 126 new workers were welcomed in Shanghai. Five years after the appeal for the Thousand it was estimated that 1,153 new workers had arrived in China under all missions. Not all, however, were men. Indeed, 672 of the number were women.

After thirty years in China the C.I.M. had 110 stations in fourteen provinces, 550 missionaries and 4,000 converts. Seven hospitals, sixteen dispensaries, and 128 opium refuges for the cure of addicts were in operation. Within the Mission the early 90's were marked by much sickness and the loss of some of the original pioneers: the pre-*Lammermuir* George Stott of Wenchow, Mrs. Meadows of the *Lammermuir* party, Dr. James Cameron, the great traveller, and Adam Dorward: Dorward travelled through Hunan for eight whole years, visiting nearly every city, without securing a permanent foothold anywhere. He died, his prayers for Hunan still unanswered. The door to Hunan was finally unlocked by Miss Jacobsen, a courageous Norwegian.

1895 marked a turning point in the work of the C.I.M. It was the end of the five-year period since the appeal of the Shanghai Conference for the Thousand, and the Mission was receiving an average of seventy additions to its ranks each year. The number of baptisms in 1895 was a record and the following year reached four figures for the first time. The sale of Scriptures likewise increased. William Cassels was consecrated first Bishop of the West China Diocese. Even the Emperor deigned to recognise Protestant missionary work for the first time by conferring the Order of the Double Dragon on eleven missionary doctors, including Dr. Douthwaite of the C.I.M. The year before, the Empress Dowager had celebrated her sixtieth birthday and the Christian women of China, to mark the occasion, presented her with an elegantly-bound New Testament in a silver casket. Not long after, the Emperor himself ordered a complete Bible.

But satisfaction at these spectacular advances was tempered by a nation-wide rising tide of anger against foreigners. There had been serious riots in 1891 and 1893 in the Yangtze valley and it was missionaries who had to bear the brunt of these attacks. In 1894 war broke out between China and Japan over the issue of the suzerainty of Korea and ended in a crushing defeat for China in April 1895. Violent repercussions everywhere followed this national humiliation. A Muslim rebellion broke out in the north-west and the Ridleys were beleaguered in Sining for seven months. In Fukien, nine Anglican missionaries were murdered. Riots in Szechwan forced sixty-five missionaries to leave the province. The riots were a spontaneous expression of popular feeling against the aggressive behaviour of the foreign powers. Chinese Christians, too, began to suffer increased persecution. Worse was to come. In 1897 two German missionaries were murdered in Shantung and by way of reprisal the Germans seized the port of Kiaochow in that province. The German action gave the cue to the other powers: in 1898 Russia, France and England all seized strategic Chinese ports. Only the United States refrained from sharing in the parcelling-out of China or the "carving up of the melon", as the Chinese called it. Little wonder that China came to associate Christianity with international banditry. H. E. Li Hung-chang, the distinguished statesman, described the Empress as "alive with wrath and angry beyond words" at these actions. Moreover, profits from the opium trade about this time amounted to £4,000,000. England was making a tawdry fortune out of China's misery. Missionary work was inevitably associated with the unscrupulous proceedings of the missionaries' compatriots. Nor were the missionaries themselves free from blame: Roman Catholics sometimes interfered in lawsuits: Protestants and Catholics alike lived comfortably amid the surrounding squalor. Some missionaries lacked the qualities which should adorn the character of ministers of the Gospel and not all were sensible or sober; there were social anomalies and continuous petty injustices which combined to aggravate the people's indignation. And the friction which clearly existed between the Roman Catholics and the Protestants was undoubtedly a stumbling block, for it was difficult to appreciate the differences between them.

To these factors must be added the fact that envy of the great technical skill and ability of Japan, the United States and Europe was creating feelings of hatred and ill-will. The Emperor and his friends saw reform as the only hope for China and in 1898 the Reform decrees were published. Among other revolutionary proposals in the decrees was one that all idol temples be closed and reopened as schools and colleges. This would have been one of the most remarkable imperial proclamations since Nebuchadnezzar, if it had gone through. The decree was actually telegraphed throughout the country and became a general talking point everywhere. But all this was too much for the conservative "Old Buddha", as the Empress was called. In a *coup d'état* she ordered the arrest of the Emperor and he became a palace prisoner although remaining on the throne. The progressive decrees were abrogated and the following year the Empress herself issued a series of inflamatory edicts in terms of great bitterness and hatred. These were posted up in every large city. Anti-foreign sentiment spread like wildfire. The reformers' demands for the modernisation of China were shelved. The coming explosion was therefore neither sudden nor unexpected; but the fatal, inevitable result of the pressure brought to bear upon China by the foreign powers. It was not so much anti-Christian as anti-foreign.

Despite the heavy clouds darkening the skies of China, missionary work went on. In 1898 Taylor initiated a forward movement into the rural areas and issued an appeal for twenty men who would be ready to forgo marriage for five years. The first advance was made in Kiangsi. Three missions opened new stations in Hunan. Dr. Charles Inwood, a Keswick Convention deputation and Miss Henrietta Soltau visited China to bring inspiration and refreshment to those engaged in the forward movement. That same year the first C.I.M. martyrdom occurred when Fleming, an evangelist to the Black Miao (Meo), was killed in Panghai, Kweichow. A year later 200 inquirers were registered there. As the century closed the C.I.M. had 700 workers in China. Thirteen thousand people had been baptised on confession of faith in the previous thirty-five years. But now events were moving to a tragic climax. Aroused by the imperial decrees public feeling was on the boil. In January 1900 the Great Powers sent a stern note to Peking calling for the suppression of a secret society whose members called themselves the Fists of Righteous Harmony (i.e. "Boxers"). But the Boxers had already gained the ear and won the favour of the Empress Dowager. In February, when they were joined by 8,000 troops, the situation deteriorated rapidly. Things were at breaking point. Both missionaries and Chinese converts were about to face an unprecedented baptism of suffering.

## CHAPTER 6

# NEW CENTURY TRAGEDY

GREAT BRITAIN entered the twentieth century in the grip of war—the Boer War. Nearly 500,000 men were in the field. Day by day the newspaper headlines scanned at Victorian breakfast tables concerned events in South Africa: the relief of Mafeking and Kimberley in February, of Bloemfontein in May and of Pretoria in June. After that guerrilla warfare was all of which the defeated Boers were capable.

But for the Church in China the twentieth century was ushered in even more sombrely dressed. Drought and three successive years of crop failures were blamed on the foreigners by the Taoist priesthood. Famine was the last straw for a nation already driven to desperation by the aggression of Western nations and Japan. The pent-up passions of the Chinese masses could no longer be contained. The Boxers, with the support of "Old Buddha", recruited a large army and promised to drive the hated barbarians out of China. The moderation of H. E. Li Hung-chang was in vain. When he urged the Empress to suppress the Boxers she became livid with anger and poured abuse upon her chief minister. On June 24th the Empress by imperial edict ordered the death of every foreigner in China. The first killings followed immediately. Foreigners in Peking all congregated in the Legation Quarter to defend themselves.

Suddenly, in July, startling headlines displaced the good news from South Africa: "Threat to kill all foreigners in China", "Chinese massacre missionaries", "Hundreds feared dead". Victorian England was horrified. Peking was cut off from the outside world. When the storm broke the majority of the 700 C.I.M. missionaries

E

in China were living at inland stations. The slaughter was worst in Shensi, Chihli and Shantung in the north, and Chekiang in the south. Of the foreigners who died 113 missionaries with their forty-six children were stationed in Shansi. A large group was killed on July 9th in Taiyuanfu, the capital, by the direct orders and in the presence of the infamous governor, Yü Hsien himself. Others died in lonely stations or as the result of unspeakable sufferings and privations endured while attempting to escape. Sixty-four of those who died in Shansi—adults and children—were connected with the C.I.M. Altogether fifty-eight C.I.M. missionaries and twenty-two children died in that dreadful year. The total death roll of foreigners was 188, including thirty-four Roman Catholics. It was thanks to H. E. Li Hung-chang and the other viceroys that the massacres did not spread.

Communications throughout the country were completely disorganised. The Post Office could not maintain its telegraph service, and the news of the terrible tragedies leaked out very slowly. The crisis was at its worst in July and August when many missionaries were making their painful way to places of safety. Some of these journeys were a record of continuous miracles.* In Peking the Japanese Chancellor and the German Ambassador were both killed in June, and on June 21st orders were given for the destruction of the Legations. Their long siege lasted for fifty-five days until they were relieved on August 14th by an international force which fought its way from Tientsin. As the allied troops arrived the Empress and her Court fled from Peking to Sian. Terrible retribution followed. The foreign soldiers burned and pillaged the beautiful imperial palaces and temples of the ancient city. The Hanlin Academy was burnt to the ground, most of its priceless treasures being destroyed. Finally H.E. Li Hung-chang was recalled and successfully negotiated the difficult settlements with the foreign powers. By October, the Boxer outbreak was at an end.

The blow was the most severe ever dealt to Protestant missions anywhere in the world. Many in the West

---

* *A Thousand Miles of Miracle*, by Glover (C.I.M.).
  *In Deaths Oft*, by C. H. S. Green (C.I.M.).

thought that the Protestant enterprise in China was finished. Of all the missions the C.I.M. suffered most both in life and in property. The British and other Governments involved naturally demanded full compensation for the sufferers. Heavy indemnities and other punitive measures were imposed on the Chinese Government. Hudson Taylor, however, with the full approval of the Mission Councils, decreed that, in conformity with the spirit of Christ, no claim at all would be made against the Chinese Government for the extensive losses of the C.I.M.: compensation, even if offered, should be refused. This decision was adopted with the Chinese Church in mind. Probably as many as 30,000 Chinese Christians—Roman Catholics and Protestants— were massacred and the survivors had suffered as terribly as the missionaries. They might have been tempted to extract what they could from a Government prepared to give compensation both to foreigners and those associated with them. Only great harm to the Church could have resulted. Although the C.I.M. action was criticised in some quarters, the British Minister in Peking warmly approved of it and sent a private donation to the Mission as an expression of his admiration and sympathy. The representative of the Chinese Foreign Office in Taiyuanfu, the Shansi capital where the greatest massacre had taken place, issued a remarkable proclamation, which was posted up in every centre where the Mission had suffered. It spoke understandingly of the Christian principles of forbearance and forgiveness which prompted the Mission's action. This proclamation benefited the cause of Christ in the province as the highest compensation could never have done.

In 1902 the Court returned, duly chastened, to Peking. It was not long before the "Old Buddha" was indulging in Court tea-parties at which Westerners were often her guests. She became a well-known figure among the foreign community. In the same year women were permitted to return to Shansi and the work of the Mission began to return to normal. The severest test of all since the Mission's foundation had thus been met and overcome.

However, the terrific strain of the Boxer crisis took its toll on the strength of the Mission's sixty-eight-year-old founder and director. In January 1899, Mr. and Mrs. Taylor had accompanied the Rev. and Mrs. Charles Inwood to a conference of west China missionaries at Chungking. Illness forced Mr. Taylor to spend the summer at Chefoo. Then in September Mr. and Mrs. Taylor paid a visit to the Mission's centres in Australia and New Zealand. In 1900 he travelled to New York to take part in the great Ecumenical Missionary Conference in April.* This Conference, held in the Carnegie Music Hall, proved to be one of the greatest assemblies in history. The President of the United States attended the opening ceremony to welcome the delegates. The audiences totalled an aggregate of over 18,000; 1,500 delegates and 800 missionaries of over 100 societies representing fifty countries, including many of the most illustrious missionaries and advocates of missions of the day, met in the closest fellowship. There were ten C.I.M. delegates. Hudson Taylor was among them, a venerable figure, feeble in health and on the verge of a breakdown. The news from China was ominous, although the storm had yet to burst, and Hudson Taylor's moving appeal for prayer for that land was one of the most memorable addresses given at the Conference. "It is not lost time to wait upon God!" was the burden of his address. The Conference concluded with the hope for a "harmonious plan of action" in the evangelisation of the world.

In 1901 Hudson Taylor made his decision to retire. The following year he appointed D. E. Hoste, distinguished member of the Cambridge Seven, and leader of the work in Shansi and Honan, as his successor. He and Mrs. Taylor then spent a year or two of happy retirement in Switzerland, until Mrs. Taylor died in 1904. The veteran now had a longing to go back to China and in

* Hudson Taylor had previously participated in the Mildmay Conference in 1878 when thirty-seven British and American societies were represented. In 1888 1,500 delegates representing 140 societies had met in the Exeter Hall, London, for a conference which was without peer in interest and importance. Hudson Taylor had again been among the platform of eminent speakers and leaders of the Church.

February 1905 Hudson Taylor set out for the Far East for the last time. His visit became a triumphal tour. On June 1st he reached Changsha, the capital of Hunan. Two days later a tea-party was given in his honour. That evening, quite suddenly and peacefully, Hudson Taylor died. There was a dramatic significance in the fact of his death in Hunan, for this was the last of the inland provinces to be opened to the Gospel. It was the province where Adam Dorward had evangelised so faithfully for eight years without visible results. As recently as 1902 two more missionaries had been murdered there. Now there were six or seven societies at work and a flourishing Christian church was emerging. Representatives from each of the societies were present at that last tea-party to do the great pioneer honour.

Hudson Taylor's death at the age of seventy-three brought to an end fifty-one years of unsparing and marvellously fruitful service to the Chinese people. The Communists today may vilify him as "the greatest imperialist of them all", but the record of his selfless labours and the tremendous material and spiritual contribution Hudson Taylor made to the common people of China speak for themselves.

## CHAPTER 7

# THE AFTERMATH

ONCE the reactionary and conservative elements in China had been defeated through the events of 1900, the country made spectacular progress. She realised that she could not ignore the scientific superiority of her Western conquerors. Old China had proved powerless against the threat from Christendom. This was the turning-point, the end of medievalism, the beginning of the end of thirty centuries of history. Educational progress was revolutionary; in 1905 a Ministry of Education was set up. Newspapers and periodicals multiplied. The Russo-Japanese war of 1904–5 and the defeat of Russia ushered in a new period in European and Asiatic history. Incidentally, this war was fought largely on Chinese soil, to the chagrin of the Chinese.

The Great Powers re-established their nationals and their trade in China. In the British House of Commons a campaign was inaugurated to bring to an end the trade in opium which had originally been introduced by the British East India Company. The devastating effect of the introduction of this drug on the economy and the moral and physical life of the Chinese can never be measured. Few more far-reaching evils can be laid at the door of the British nation than this. Very gradually the conscience of the nation was awakened, and after a long struggle the Government finally decided on May 7th, 1913 to bring the trade in opium to an end. Significantly, a week of prayer for China was held in Great Britain in 1906 and another memorable day of prayer on April 27th, 1913, just preceding the Government's decision. It was none too early.

The atmosphere left by the events of 1900 was

scarcely favourable for preaching the Gospel, particularly by those from countries which had reduced China to complete subjection. But strangely enough there was a changed attitude to Christianity. Suddenly it became mildly popular to be a Christian. There was a passion for education and the young flocked to Christian schools. Dr. Timothy Richard's name was prominently linked with this educational progress and the new lease of life it gave to China. The percentage of Christians in China has never been great, but in the early years of the new century there was a marked increase in the number of conversions. The new pro-Christian movement began in the west, in the province of Szechwan. Wealthy Chinese contributed towards the construction of Christian churches and buildings were often offered free to bewildered missionaries. The work of the C.I.M. experienced a spectacular outward growth, both in Szechwan and elsewhere. In 1885 the total of annual baptisms had been only 400; in 1895 the figure had risen to 700; in 1905 it reached 2,500 and continued to mount in the following years. But among the converts were not a few who joined the Church with ulterior motives. Twenty years later these "rice Christians" were one of the greatest hindrances to the Church's further growth. But probably the Chinese Church as a whole suffered most in this way as the result of the new emphasis on education. Even before 1900 several Christian colleges and universities, including St. John's University, Shanghai, had been opened. The tremendous demand for Western education after 1900 led to the opening of many Christian schools, colleges and universities. An increasing percentage of the missionary force became engaged in educational work. The original strongly evangelistic emphasis of the Christian Mission was lost. Education rather than conversion seemed to be the aim.

But movements of spiritual revival also began in many parts of China. The Rev. Jonathan Goforth, after sharing in the great awakening in Korea, carried the message throughout Manchuria and into China proper in 1908 and 1909. Shansi, the tortured province, was visited, and among the Chinese whose lives were revolutionised was a young evangelist, Wang Chi-tai, who in partnership with Albert Lutley of the C.I.M. became a great power for God in his own province and then throughout north and west China. Remarkable results accompanied his campaigns and the churches received a fresh impartation of life and power. In his report of the work in the west China diocese for 1910, Bishop Cassels wrote in warmly appreciative terms of the profound effect this movement of revival had had on the churches of the diocese. Other men who had a powerful ministry were Hsieh Meng-tzi of Anhwei and Dr. Yao of Kiangsi.

.    .    .

As with mountain climbers, so with missionaries, there is a fever in their blood for the unconquered. Paul wanted to preach Christ where He was not named. For the C.I.M. Tibet presented an obvious target. Cameron made the first spectacular journey in 1877. In 1888 Cecil Polhill Turner of the Cambridge Seven and his wife tried to approach Tibetan nomads from the northwest based on Sining. There he studied Tibetan under a Mongol who had accompanied Hué and Gabbet to Lhasa. In 1892 a gallant woman by the name of Annie Taylor, after a year in Sikkim learning Tibetan, made an unprecedented journey into Tibet from the east with Lhasa as her goal. Her party was attacked by bandits several times, losing most of their possessions and some of the pack animals, but she courageously ventured on and only just failed to reach her destination. In 1897 the Polhill Turners moved south to settle in the border town of Tatsienlu, where half the population is Tibetan. Several recruits joined them and they embarked on long and arduous journeys in every direction with the one purpose of making Christ known. There was a temporary pause in this activity during the Boxer crisis until Huston Edgar took up the work. The first four converts were baptised in 1904 and eight more the following year. Cunningham joined Edgar and Batang was occupied, only to be abandoned again when the 1911 Revolution broke out, but not before many a long and fascinating evangelistic journey had been made to several large Tibetan towns, including Litang.

.    .    .

Chinese Turkestan is another area which has an irresistible lure for the traveller and the missionary pioneer. Sinkiang, as it is now called, extends 1,100 miles from east to west, bordering Russia in the north and Tibet and India in the south. Prior to 1905 Swedish missionaries working at Yarkand and Kashgar in the extreme west were the only Protestant missionaries in the whole area. Most of the province is a barren desert surrounded by lofty mountains. Its ancient cities, now buried beneath the sands of the Gobi, speak of prosperous times long ago. Today the greatly-reduced population of several millions consists of Chinese, Turkis, Mongols, Manchus, Sarts and Hindus, living at widely scattered oases. Islam is the prevailing religion. As early as 1888 two C.I.M. missionaries had travelled extensively in Sinkiang, circulating Scriptures in six different languages. But it was not until 1905 that anyone took up permanent residence there. In that year George Hunter made his first visit to Hami and Urumchi, the capital, now called Tihwa. In 1906 Urumchi became his base and his home. There he remained with only one furlough for most of the remaining forty years of his life. He completely identified himself with the people, who grew to love and respect this tall Highlander. As the result of untiring journeys selling the Scriptures and preaching the Gospel he acquired an unequalled knowledge of Central Asia. In 1907 Hunter was urged to visit Shanghai to attend the Centenary of Missions Conference. But no one there seemed interested in the wealth of information and experience he possessed about the unevangelised regions he represented. Two weeks in Shanghai after the close of the Conference were enough of civilisation for him and he returned to his lonely outpost from which he did not emerge again until 1931. For ten years he lived alone, seeing no foreigners save the occasional scientist and traveller who called to inquire on all manner of subjects from the best-informed European in Central Asia. Learned men honoured him, and many whose names are world-famous would acknowledge that they had learned much from this plain pioneer missionary. In 1932 the Consul-General in Kashgar handed to him the Order of the M.B.E. which King George V had been pleased to confer on him. Long before this Dr. Morison, the well-known traveller and the Peking correspondent of *The Times* had written the following tribute: "In Urumchi one Englishman has made his home, Mr. G. W. Hunter of the China Inland Mission. One of the most widely travelled men in the province . . . he takes rank with the most distinguished and tactful pioneer missionaries sent by England to China . . ."

. . .

In the south-west, Judd and Broumton first observed the Miao (Meo) tribes in 1877 and Hudson Taylor began to pray for their evangelisation. When James Adam went to work in Anshun in 1888 he was immediately attracted to these simple and picturesque people. The first Miao converts were baptised in 1898 and the first chapel erected the following year. The nearest thing to a mass movement ever to take place in China now began. Large numbers of the Miao tribe from 250 villages began to visit Anshun, all eager for Christian instruction. Twenty more were baptised in 1902. As they believed sorcerers burned their wands and the people their charms. In 1903 Adam met a party of men belonging to the Big Flowery Miao in the mountains returning from a wild boar hunt and was immediately invited to their village of Kopu, several days' journey away. Within three years a church of 250 members arose. In 1904 the Gospel spread like a prairie fire to the Miao in Yunnan where Samuel Pollard of the United Methodist Mission was soon overwhelmed with the task of teaching the hundreds of inquirers. A church of 4,000 members was built up in the Methodist field alone. In 1906 1,480 tribal believers were baptised in the Anshun area; less than 1 per cent of the first 5,000 converts fell away. The movement spread farther and farther west until it reached the tribes living in the Mekong and Salween valleys. In 1907 the Yunnan Miao reached out to the Lisu. The next year the Lisu carried the Gospel to the Lahu. In 1910 the Miao sought to evangelise the Kopu. In that year the Nosu, relations of the Lisu, the Shan and the Chungkia were also reached. In 1906 there were nearly 2,000 converts. Bible translation was the first task of the missionaries. Adam made a translation in romanised script, while Pollard invented the "Pollard Script". The coming of Christianity meant a radical renewal of tribal life: spirit worship and drunkenness, opium smoking and prostitution disappeared. Daily services were held, chapels were built and Bible Schools established.

.    .    .

In 1893 a cultured young lady who had been brought up in France went to China with the C.I.M. She worked in Shansi for seven years and barely escaped with her life in the Boxer troubles. Her names was Eva French. In 1901 she was joined by Mildred Cable. The two ladies went to Hwochow in Shansi where they built up an extensive educational and evangelistic work. Mildred Cable re-started the school for girls which had originally been opened in 1883—one of the first of its kind in China. In 1908 Francesca French joined her sister and the renowned "Trio" worked together for the rest of their lives.

.    .    .

The first decade of the twentieth century was thus one of great growth and expansion for the Chinese Church. In 1910 the C.I.M. had founded 611 organised churches throughout China with a total of over 20,000 communicant members. Missionaries totalled 933. The decade had seen the death of the Mission's founder and the appointment of D. E. Hoste, a comparatively youthful leader. Not a few gloomy prophets foretold an early collapse of the Mission after the founder's death, believing that it was built on his personality. If so and if the Mission was not of God, this would undoubtedly have happened. But the change in leadership made no difference to the character and the traditions of the Mission. Its members were still strong in faith, fired with the ambition to reach every part of China with the Gospel and to establish churches firmly rooted in the Word of God, strong enough to face the storms of the coming years.

. . .

The most significant of all the ecumenical conferences up to date was held in 1910. Five hundred delegates each from Great Britain and the United States and 200 from the continent of Europe met in Edinburgh. They came as representatives of missionary societies and not of churches. The C.I.M. was again well represented. Dr. Robert Speer gave the opening address and Dr. John Mott the closing one on "The Evangelisation of the world in this generation". Hitherto the ecumenical idea had been fostered entirely by evangelical missionary groups, which recognised a true spiritual unity and sought a closer co-operation in their work on these grounds. This was a practical and Biblical ideal. But the movement took a new turning in 1910. The denominational church leaders adopted the idea of unity and gave it a new objective. They began to envisage some form of church union and a committee was set up to study the problems involved. Fifty-five years later the problems are still being studied. Whereas the Christian Church was once divided only vertically into denominations, it has, since 1910, become even more seriously divided horizontally by theological liberalism—a line which runs through all the denominations. Theological liberalism and not denominationalism is the really divisive factor today. Spiritual unity, centred on the Person and Work of Christ and based on loyalty to the Word of God, has a clear theological warrant and must be fostered by all possible means.

Looking at the world of their day, the delegates at Edinburgh were full of optimism. There was universal peace. The unevangelised areas of the globe were governed either by Christian colonial powers or by Governments favourable to Christianity. Missions were prospering and everything seemed to point to the early completion of the task of evangelising the world. The delegates little realised how these hopes were to be disappointed and how near the whole world was to a series of disasters which would alter the whole course of history in a direction unfavourable to the Christian faith and missionary expansion. In China the decade which had begun in tragedy and political turmoil was to end in revolution.

CHAPTER 8

# AN EMPIRE CRUMBLES

IN 1910 a Chinese almost unknown to the West was kidnapped in London's West End. Dr. Sun Yat Sen was regarded by the Imperial Embassy officials as a dangerous revolutionary—which he was. As early as 1895 he had memorialised the throne and helped to encourage reform societies in China. The Embassy therefore kept him under guard in the Chinese Embassy in Portland Place (now the London office of the Communist Chinese Chargé d'affaires). The intention was to smuggle Dr. Sun back to China and place him out of harm's way. Dr. Sun was a Christian and had been baptised as a boy in Honolulu before returning to China in 1885. Later he tried to foment a revolutionary spirit from Japan and then from Annam and there were frequent abortive uprisings in China. He was visiting London to gain support from Chinese living in Great Britain when he was arrested. As it happened he had a missionary doctor friend in the city, Sir James Cantlie, so he hopefully dropped a note out of his window addressed to his friend. Happily the note was picked up and delivered. Dr. Sun's imprisonment was reported and his release secured. Thus he lived to see the fulfilment of his dreams in the nationalist revolution. In March 1911 a major uprising took place in Canton, causing the death of seventy-two members of Dr. Sun's party. But the revolution spread to Wuchang, Shanghai and Nanking and the date associated with the revolution is the tenth day of the tenth month of 1911—the Double Tenth.

The Empress Dowager and her son had already died within a day of each other in November 1908. When the revolution took place the heir to the Dragon Throne was

Henry Pu-yi, a boy of only five-and-a-half years of age. A dynasty which had begun in 1644 thus tottered to its fall. Dr. Sun Yat Sen was sworn in in January 1912 as the first provisional President and the first Christian Supreme Ruler of China. He once expressed the opinion that "the awakening of China actually began when Robert Morrison translated the Bible into Chinese". Six weeks later Dr. Sun gave way to Yuan Shih-kai, a well-known general. But the new era was no more favourable to the progress of Christianity than the old Manchu dynasty. Following the formal abdication of the Manchus on February 12th, 1912, a fearful reign of terror ensued. Settled government was virtually suspended. Some of the loveliest and wealthiest cities of China were ravaged by criminal and lawless elements. Missions did not escape. Two missionaries and six children of a C.I.M. associate mission were murdered in Sian. Several stations were looted and many only narrowly escaped death. The consular authorities advised the evacuation of all missionaries but the majority were able to remain at their stations, where they disarmed opposition by engaging in Red Cross work and the care of destitute refugees. On occasions they even became intermediaries between the opposing forces. As in former times of crisis the favourable impression made by these services inclined many to the Christian faith.

The new situation created by the revolution opened wider still the hitherto half-closed doors to the spread of the Gospel. The official classes expressed an interest in Christianity. English Bible study groups held in missionaries' homes were widely used to attract officials and scholars. The rejection of the old Confucian ethics left a vacuum which was hard to fill. Licence and anarchy threatened to succeed the years of despotism. President Yuan Shih-kai in his inauguration address in 1912 said, "The greatest need of the nation can be summed up in one word—morality . . . for no nation can stand save upon the eternal verities which underlie right and wrong." The Christian Church seized the opportunity. Never before had such quantities of Christian literature been distributed throughout China. Millions of copies of the Scriptures were sold. City walls and gates carried tens of thousands of Gospel posters. Every effort was made to reach the masses with the Good News of Jesus Christ and the response was tremendous. In 1911 and 1912 through the work of the C.I.M. alone between 9,000 and 10,000 were baptised. Church buildings had to be enlarged as some congregations exceeded 1,000. A thousand C.I.M. missionaries and associates with 2,500 Chinese colleagues were working in 1,200 centres.

This sudden popularity, however, proved to be deleterious in certain respects. The rapid multiplication of Christian schools ranging from primary schools to universities of the highest academic standard brought very large numbers of Chinese young people under Christian influence. The demand for the best available education gave to Christian schools a growing prestige. There were five fine Christian universities. Missions led the way, too, in medical and scientific work. The renowned and beautiful Peking Union Medical College was established and staffed largely by Western doctors. Many of China's future leaders were being educated in these Christian institutions. "But these students were little interested in the question of personal salvation," says Bishop Stephen Neill. "How can China live anew? was the burning question. Those who were baptised had almost no interest in the Church, though they were loyal to Christ as far as they understood it." Bishop Stephen Neill sums up the situation in the words: "The Gospel was presented to the Chinese people less as a Gospel of personal salvation than as a means of political and social salvation." Education in Christian institutions provided more political leaders than church leaders. It certainly popularised the liberal brand of Christianity which undermined the young Church's faith and paved the way for the coming of Communism.

The C.I.M., along with some other missions, continued to emphasise direct and widespread evangelism more than educational work. The churches were encouraged to operate their own primary schools and the Mission provided a few high schools, but these were mainly for the benefit of the children of Christians. One of the products of a C.I.M. school in Szechwan was Dr. James Yen, the distinguished pioneer of mass education in China.

Greater emphasis was laid by the C.I.M. on the training of Christian leaders. Bible schools where evangelists and pastors were trained to work in the rural churches throughout the Mission's field were set up. This was a plan which Hudson Taylor had had in mind at a very early date. In Shansi, a Bible Institute was opened which trained hundreds of men and women evangelists at their own expense. Dreyer was the first principal. A "floating Bible School", under the direction of Dr. Keller, endeavoured to evangelise the 22 million of Hunan; itinerant bands of students—"Biola Bands" (sponsored by the Bible Institute of Los Angeles)—travelled up and down the waterways of the province, the students studying and witnessing at the same time. Similar Bible-training institutes were established in Chekiang, Szechwan and Kiangsi, while a Women's Bible School in Shansi was conducted by Miss Mildred Cable and the Misses French. Missionaries shared a growing awareness that the future of the Chinese Church would depend on the quality of its leadership.

Medical work continued to feature in the C.I.M. programme. The founder was himself a doctor and convinced of its value. High standards were maintained in all the hospitals and dispensaries which provided a first-class service of which the Chinese were quick to avail themselves. In 1913 twenty-seven C.I.M. doctors were operating nine hospitals and sixty-eight dispensaries, mostly in remote areas where no other medical services existed. On January 15th, 1913 President Yuan Shih-kai personally addressed the China Medical Missionary Association and expressed his gratitude for the charitable services rendered by medical missionaries, especially in the interior of the country. C.I.M. associate Missions also conducted orphanages, industrial schools and schools for the blind.

In 1914, of 2 million "Christians" in China, five out of six were Roman Catholics. The Protestants, however, were generally speaking better-educated and more influential than the Catholics.

F

The outbreak of the First World War in 1914 profoundly affected the work of missions in China but did not interrupt it. Japan sided with the Western allies and captured Kiaochow from the Germans. But she also took advantage of the world situation to make crushing demands on China, backed up by an ultimatum which China had no alternative to accepting. The first world conflict was a profound shock to the non-Christian world. The "heathen" looked on while "Christian nations" fought each other to the death!

Nevertheless, opportunities abounded for preaching the Gospel. There seemed to be a greater liberty for religious propaganda. Chinese "evangelisation societies" sprang up in Shansi and elsewhere. Sherwood Eddy held a number of outstanding evangelistic campaigns for university students. For the C.I.M. 1914 was the most fruitful year in its history and over 5,000 baptisms took place. The number of Chinese evangelists working with the Mission was nearly 1,700, twice the number ten years earlier. But forces of reaction were also at work, and there was some return to idolatry after the revolutionary iconoclasm. Confucius worship was revived.

1915 was the Jubilee Year of the C.I.M. Like a huge banyan-tree the Mission had struck roots throughout the whole of China. Its growth from a small seed had been phenomenal. Among its international fellowship were workers from all the countries of the English-speaking world and from Finland, Russia, Belgium, Holland, Germany, Austria, Sweden, Norway, Denmark, Switzerland, Italy, Sicily and India. There were 1,327 mission stations and outstations and 372 schools. During the first twenty-five years of the Mission's history there had been less than 5,000 baptisms, but in the second twenty-five years there were over 45,000. Since the commencement of the work and the opening of an account with £10, more than £750,000 had been contributed. The only explanation of these facts is that the work was God's—begun by Him, continued by Him and blessed by Him. Through faith Hudson Taylor had attempted and achieved the impossible: in 1865 there was no Christian church anywhere in the interior of China: in

1915 churches of many missions existed in every province and in Manchuria, Mongolia and Turkestan; hundreds of thousands of children and students were receiving education in Christian schools and universities; many hospitals were ministering to the sick and many young Chinese were being trained for the Christian ministry. In this achievement, the C.I.M. had been the pioneer. Now they were merely partners with many others in this stupendous undertaking. But the task was far from complete. There were still many unreached millions and the Church was scarcely beyond its infancy. If the Church was to be brought to maturity and made strong enough to survive the travail of the coming years, much remained to be done.

## CHAPTER 9

# RED STAR RISES

THE fierce storms which threatened the first large party of C.I.M. missionaries as they voyaged towards China in 1866 did not compare with the violent tempests which threatened the now extensive work of the Mission in the years following the celebration of its Jubilee.

Hopeless failure marked the first four years of the Republic and deeply disappointed the Chinese people. In 1915 Yuan Shih-kai decided in desperation to set up a constitutional monarchy with himself as emperor—to no avail. In 1916 he died, leaving the country in the throes of civil strife. China has never recovered. Following the civil war between the old régime and the revolutionaries, Yuan's action sparked off war between himself and the other war-lords. In 1917, after Yuan's death, the situation was more serious than at any time since 1911. The young Emperor himself was restored to the throne for a fleeting twelve days but this only provoked violent hostilities.

At last the Great War came to an end. But the Versailles Peace Conference was a bitter disappointment to China. She had hoped to wrest from Germany her rights over the province of Shantung, but instead these were transferred to her enemy Japan. The Chinese delegates left the conference table in disgust and refused to sign the Treaty. And on the basis of this disgust Sun Yat Sen in Canton built up his new revolutionary Government.

Moreover, Communism arose out of the European war. The long-heralded Communist Revolution actually took place in 1917 in a major country. Russia immediately made friendly gestures to China, while other European nations were continuing to treat her as a form of colonial territory. Public opinion reacted favourably.

China began to look to Russia. Young Chinese began to visit Russia for their education and for advanced military training. A rising spirit of resistance against foreign dictation and not least against Japan, against whom boycotts were organised, was manifested. The students of Peking became increasingly vocal and active in demonstrating against foreign infringements of China's rights. The student-led May the Fourth Movement had great significance for missions because it was essentially an anti-foreign intellectual movement directed to a renaissance of Chinese culture. In so far as Christianity was foreign it lost caste in the eyes of young Chinese. It had always been a "foreign religion" in the eyes of the Chinese people, but this term now took on a new significance. The movement gradually became a demonstration of national feeling within the urban class and in 1921 led to the formation of the Chinese Communist Party. Thereby China's eventual fate and the fate of foreign missions were sealed.

From 1921 onwards, war between the newly-constituted revolutionary Government in Canton under Sun Yat Sen and the Government in the north was incessant. By 1922, the authority of the Central Government had virtually ceased. Instead of one Government there were almost twenty. During the year six different Cabinets tried to rule. Two of the premiers were Christians. But the whole country was in the grip of the military factions. In Szechwan alone there were at one time four contending armies. Soldiers swarmed over China's eighteen provinces like a plague of locusts. Millions of armed men had to maintain themselves with no proper Government support, and they had no alternative but to live on the people. The soldiers were often lawless, extortionate and brutal. The long-suffering people of China lived in fear and under their constant oppression.

But this was not the whole story of China's misery. In the general state of lawlessness, innumerable bands of brigands, bandits and robbers composed of soldier deserters and the most evil elements in society pillaged and plundered at will, sacking and looting cities and behaving with a cruelty and wickedness which baffle description. As time went on these illegal armies, many of them Communist-led, grew in size and became increasingly audacious. Chinese were murdered or kidnapped and held to ransom in increasing numbers. Property was wantonly destroyed, including that of many missionary societies. No province escaped. The gloom was unrelieved. In 1923 commercial steamers on the Yangtze were fired on frequently. The famous Blue Express from Shanghai to Peking was derailed and 135 foreign passengers were taken away for ransom.

Nature, too, seemed unfriendly. Disastrous floods rendered millions destitute. The 1920 earthquakes in the north-west made 100,000 people homeless, and in 1925 there was another devastating earthquake in the region of Tali in the south-west. Drought in 1920 caused famine in Hopeh on a staggering scale and twelve C.I.M. missionaries were appointed for relief work. By 1922 eight provinces were affected. Pneumonic plague. Bubonic plague. Cholera. Typhoons. All contributed to the total misery.

Almost the greatest curse was the recrudescence of opium-growing and addiction. This scourge had been well on the way to being controlled if not wiped out in 1916. Actual poppy growing had ceased. But by 1919 its cultivation was again widespread and opium addicts were multiplying. Misery followed in the train of the habit. The greed of officials and war-lords, who controlled nine-tenths of the export of drugs, and incredible corruption, were responsible for this disaster.

How could missionary work continue under such impossible conditions? But the C.I.M., with a persistent passion for the impossible, maintained varied activities in the most exposed places and in the face of constant danger. Its missionaries intimately shared the perils of the epoch with the Chinese. They were present to bring relief where famine, flood and earthquake wrought havoc. Its Mission compounds were often opened to protect women and children refugees from marauding brigand bands or troops of one of the warring armies. In 1924 six foreigners were killed and others kidnapped or held to ransom, including members of the C.I.M. Mission stations were sacked, looted and damaged. Dangers increased with the growing anarchy.

In 1919 of the eleven C.I.M. hospitals, the newest was the hospital and leprosy centre in Lanchow: the Borden Memorial Hospital, built in memory of the young American millionaire, a Harvard University graduate who died in Egypt on his way to serve among the Muslims of the north-west of China. In the leprosy wing of this hospital probably more Muslims and Tibetans confessed Christ than anywhere else in China. In 1924 another hospital was opened at Hochow, the strongest Muslim centre in China, north-west from Lanchow. The Mission's hospitals were almost always filled with wounded soldiers, among whom a very fruitful work was done.

Year by year many remarkable conversions took place among men and women of all classes of society. In the stormy years between 1909 and 1918, C.I.M. missionaries baptised a total of 40,000 converts. During the turbulent 20's an average of between 5,000 and 6,000 baptisms a year was maintained. Each one who confessed Christ in this way was an individual miracle of God's saving grace.

But in addition to the extensive opportunities for evangelism, the need was never lost sight of for consolidating the churches and for training Chinese leaders. In east Szechwan the Paoning Cathedral had been consecrated in 1914. In 1916 a Diocesan training college had been started and in 1922 Bishop Howard Mowll was consecrated in Canterbury as assistant to Bishop Cassels. The Central Bible Training Institute in Shansi, and the Bible institutes in Hangchow and Nanchang were training hundreds of laymen and evangelists. In Hunan Dr. Keller's students continued their unique work, the Biola Bands visiting 100,000 homes in 1916.

Provincial church conferences had first been held as early as 1914, 1915 and 1916 in several provinces. In 1918 the three Protestant missions working in Kansu held a united conference at the Borden Memorial Hospital. At these conferences missionaries and Chinese began to face together the problems of self-support, church evangelism, marriage and funeral ceremonies, Seventh Day Adventism and the Tongues question, which were exercising the churches. The churches were also experiencing a new inflow of life through the ministry of outstanding Chinese and missionary evangelists and teachers. Hsieh Meng-tzi of Anhwei was welcomed all over China by the churches; Ting Li-mei was another widely-used servant of God, while Jessie Gregg and Charlotte Tippett of the C.I.M. were much used among the women of China in many provinces and in Manchuria.

Several notable individual missionary achievements must not escape mention: Miss Susie Garland invented a Braille system in Chinese; Fred Baller completed the revision of the Union Version Old Testament after seventeen years of work; in Kansu Dr. Parry received the thanks of the local authorities for stamping out an outbreak of pneumonic plague.

1922 was a red-letter year in the history of the Chinese Church. Following the Edinburgh Conference of 1910, a Continuation Committee met in Shanghai in 1913. It represented the Protestant forces in China, a third of its membership being Chinese. The Committee met regularly and in 1922 decided to call a National Christian Conference. A thousand delegates representing almost every Protestant body then working in China gathered in Shanghai. At least a third of the delegates were Chinese. The C.I.M., having the largest group of churches in China, was well represented by both missionaries and Chinese. The Conference marked a stage in the transition from "foreign missions" to the "Chinese Church". In spite of the growing threat of liberal theology general satisfaction was felt among the evangelical representatives with the official loyalty to the central truths of the Gospel expressed in the Conference publication *The Christian Message*. Although the C.I.M. shared enthusiastically in this as in all previous ecumenical conferences, enthusiasm waned some years later over the movement to amalgamate the churches of China under the "Church of Christ in China". The theological issues had by then become acute. This body, in spite of the abstention of the C.I.M. churches, the Anglican Church, the Lutheran Church, the Methodists and most Baptists, became by its union, the second largest group of Protestant Christians in China. The largest group of churches was still that associated with the C.I.M.

The Communists seemed to regard the 1922 Conference as a challenge. The attacks on the Church became increasingly bitter. Under the guidance of Borodin, the experienced Russian propagandist, who arrived in 1923 to advise the revolutionary Government in Canton, the Communist propaganda machine was set in full swing. A flood of anti-foreign and anti-Christian literature simply poured from the presses. In this propaganda the intelligentsia of China were prominent. The type of Christian education that had been so popular was partly to blame. Truth had been so mixed with error, evangelism with imperialism and Christianity with politics that even sincere Christians hardly knew what to believe. An analysis of 97 pamphlets showed that 36 were directed against Christian education, 34 against Christianity generally, 11 against Christians, 5 against the Church, 5 against missionaries, 3 against Jesus Christ Himself, 2 against Christian literature and 1 against the Bible. A large number of political societies of a Left-wing or Communist character were formed. Mass meetings and great demonstrations were organised throughout the country, aiming to poison the people's minds against Christianity. Not unnaturally, this anti-foreign propaganda had its effect on the churches and some began to declare their independence of foreign missionary organisations.

In 1924 Marshal Feng Yü-Hsiang, the "Christian General" with the well-behaved, hymn-singing army, seized Peking. Across the tragic stage of China there strutted many a strange figure, and non more enigmatic than Marshal Feng. A Communist-inspired riot in Canton caused damage by fire to the extent of £2,000,000 and the loss of many lives. Although this resulted in the expulsion of all Soviet agents, Sun Yat Sen nevertheless signed a Treaty with Soviet Russia.

1925 was the Diamond Jubilee of the Mission. For

sixty years the Mission had survived massacres, revolutions, riots and constant opposition. New reinforcements had arrived in a constant supply to replace those who retired or who died in battle. But there were still 2 of the Eighteen (1875), 12 of the Seventy (1881) and 17 of the Hundred (1887) serving on the field! With God's blessing 54,000 baptisms took place during the decade after 1915. The mission worked from 260 central stations. Organised churches numbered 1,238, and there were 3,843 Chinese workers, most of whom were voluntary.

The story of the financial provision for the work over the past ten years was most remarkable. If ever the Mission was called upon to test the promises contained in God's Word, it was during those years of war and world-wide upheaval. As the conflict dragged to its close the exchange rate in China became very unfavourable. But God's way of countering the unfavourable exchange rate was to increase the general income, and this amid the economic distress. Moreover, the highest contribution continued to come from Great Britain, in spite of her wartime impoverishment. In 1920 the British contribution was actually twice that of North America. During the five years of war in Europe, God moved His stewards to give £500,000, which brought the total to £2,500,000 since the beginning of the work. Thus the income during the First World War instead of diminishing was virtually doubled! When peace returned widespread unemployment and economic distress prevailed throughout the world. China was in chaos and the rate of exchange was so unfavourable that not a few business houses in the Far East were ruined. Humanly speaking the maintenance of over 1,000 C.I.M. missionaries was economically impossible! And it cannot be denied that there were times of great testing for the members of the Mission, especially in 1921. The strictest economy had to be practised as the cost of living rose steeply. But in 1925, it was possible to acknowledge the goodness of God in sending £1,400,000 in the ten years since the Jubilee year in 1915. In this marvellous way the needs of a very large family of missionaries were met. God had prepared Hudson Taylor for the founding of the Mission by severe trials and testings in the matter of finance; without them his faith and character could never have gained the necessary strength and fibre to found and lead the Mission. In the same way, each generation of his followers has had to learn through the same kind of experiences. It is not enough to live on a tradition; each new member has had to learn how to contribute his own quota of living, up-to-date faith. That faith was about to be tested in other ways than financial.

## CHAPTER 10

# THE GREAT EVACUATION

1925 is known as the year of China's challenge to the foreign powers. Sun Yat Sen died in Peking—a Christian to the end—and rifts began to appear in his hitherto united Party. It was clear that the Communists were determined at any cost to command for themselves alone. On the island of Whampoa in the West River estuary, Chiang Kai-shek was meanwhile forging his own instrument in the Whampoa Academy, where he had been placed in command. On May 30th a student agitator was shot by a British policeman in the International Settlement in Shanghai. This was as a spark to powder and kindled a blaze of anti-foreign bitterness which swept throughout the length and breadth of the land. The years of utter frustration and pent-up feelings for the Chinese people were suddenly given violent expression. The Chinese Government demanded the revision of the Treaties and the Washington Agreement paved the way for negotiations in Peking. As anti-foreign passions were inflamed, the tale of suffering also increased. It was clear that the main force of the second revolution was being directed at the foreigner and not at social conditions: kidnapping and killing were the order of the day. Six more missionaries were killed during the year. Missionaries became the object of vilification from every quarter, most of it Communist-inspired. Misunderstanding, misrepresentation and intentional ill-will were their daily lot and situations were created which could only be met in the spirit of Jesus Christ, whether the accusations were just or unjust. The painful experiences of these years called for infinite patience and forbearance. In the last written words of Bishop Cassels before his death in

1925 he said, "We came in the steps of Him who was despised and rejected of men. Perhaps this is one of the lessons we have to learn at a time when extraordinary and bitter hatred is being stirred up against us."

It can scarcely be said that the Church was really "anti-foreign". Rather was it "pro-Chinese" for it was natural for the Christians to see events from a Chinese point of view. The history of relations between China and the West was open to the worst possible interpretation. It could not be denied that Christian missions were the first to take advantage of the permission to travel and to reside in the interior, a permission which China had been forced to concede as the result of defeat in war. It was easy to believe that missionaries were agents in the pay of foreign Governments and a kind of "spearhead of cultural aggression". Chinese Christians could scarcely be expected to appreciate the sacrifices which missionaries made when even the humblest mission station was to them an evidence of wealth and power. "Imagine us not exposed to danger," wrote one missionary, "but misunderstood by those we seek to serve, drinking the cup of ingratitude, shame, humiliation and reproach, despised by the many and hated by some. We are partakers of the fellowship of Christ's sufferings and learning when reviled not to revile again."

The bandit armies, increasingly Communist-inspired, determined to exploit the lawlessness and the misery of the people. It is remarkable that despite the prevailing conditions the Mission welcomed no less than sixty-nine recruits to China in 1925. In spite of all the anti-Christian feeling abroad, 4,577 individuals dared to make a public confession of Christ in baptism. Among them was a cultured scholar working in a district *yamen*, a young man of striking and prepossessing personality, but burdened with a sense of need. He had tried every avenue of Chinese philosophy in his search for the meaning of life and then had explored Western philosophy with equally disappointing results. He procured a Bible but its simple style offended his classical and scholarly taste. Nevertheless after studying its teaching for several weeks with a C.I.M. missionary he clearly believed. "Why have

I never heard this before? Why has this message not been preached in China? This is more wonderful than anything!" His sadness slipped away and, his prejudice against the Mandarin Bible overcome, he became an avid reader. Naturally he found the truth about the Resurrection of the body a difficulty but he now distrusted his unaided reason and humbly believed the mystery. He was a transformed man, a representative of the deep pulsing heart of China—one of the many truly hungering and thirsting after righteousness in a nation struggling to be born.

In 1926 passions were further inflamed when the British Navy sailed up the Yangtze Gorges and bombarded the populous city of Wanhsien, killing many and doing heavy damage. Foreigners were ordered out of the city, including the C.I.M. missionaries. Many churches all over China decided to sever their relations with all foreigners. Communist-inspired newspapers hurled all kinds of abuse and indulged in every imaginable calumny against the foreigner, be he merchant or missionary. Marshall Feng, the so-called "Christian General", paid a prolonged visit to Moscow to study Soviet theory and thenceforth was more disposed to Communism than to Christianity.

Finding the national situation utterly intolerable, the southern armies commenced their long-planned march to the north in August. They now intended to unify the country by force. Chiang Kai-shek was the Commander. They quickly captured Hankow and Hanyang in September and Wuchang fell in December. This move was accompanied by nation-wide demonstrations and boycotts, and the foreign consuls advised missionaries in the south and south-west of China to withdraw to places of safety. But in 200 C.I.M. stations missionaries carried on, even in brigand-infested Honan. Two Gospel boats in Kiangsu sold more Scriptures than ever before. A record number visited the Reading Room in Yangchow and 300 Bibles were sold. In the southern part of Kiangsi where armies were always marching, the opportunities to preach to the soldiers were unprecedented. The church was often filled, to the amazement of the scoffers, and at one time every officer in the city was presented with the claims of Christ. There was continued progress among the tribes. The two old-established churches at Wenchow and Pingyang in Chekiang were handed over to the Chinese leaders. Together they had ninety country churches and during the year there were 153 baptisms in these two places alone. Even in tragic Wanhsien the Christians remained steadfast in spite of fierce persecution. Financially it was also a good year for the C.I.M. and the first year in which the receipts from North America exceeded those from Great Britain, where the financial depression was at its height. In spite of the adverse circumstances the total of baptisms mounted.

As 1927 opened, all eyes watched the southern armies which seemed to be rapidly sweeping everything before them. Aided by foreign advisers, both in the field and in highly-organised propaganda, they overran all resistance. On January 3rd, as the armies crossed the Yangtze the crowds rioted in the British Concession at Hankow. On March 21st the Southerners entered the Chinese city of Shanghai which was given over to massacre and pillage. Unless a Defence Force had already come out from Great Britain to defend the International Settlements, the same fate would have overtaken them. When Nanking fell on March 24th, several foreigners were amongst the many killed. The British Minister in Peking promptly requested that all missionaries be recalled from the interior; similar instructions were received from the American authorities. April 3rd, 1927 was therefore a very dark day. There were altogether 1,185 C.I.M. missionaries in China. How was their withdrawal possible? Where would the money come from? Where could they be accommodated? How could they persuade isolated missionaries of the necessity of evacuation? What of the leaderless and penniless schools and churches? It might take some workers two months to reach the coast and the dangers on the way would be great. But the decision was made and within an hour telegrams were dispatched to the more distant provinces and letters to those more quickly reached, advising the workers to follow the official instructions. The journeys to the coast alone cost nearly £4,000 and the many passages home an added £10,000. Yet all the money needed was available when required.

The clouds gathered as the year wore on. The material losses suffered by the Mission were immense. Mission premises were occupied, looted and often destroyed. The Hudson Taylor school in Szechwan was entirely destroyed and would cost at least £10,000 to replace. The Language School in Yangchow was wrecked. The large hospital in Kaifeng was a total loss. Indeed the damage to property alone was calculated at £50,000. But the human losses were even greater. Morris Slichter and his three-year-old daughter were shot dead by brigands while evacuating from their station in Kweichow and Mrs. Slichter wounded and held prisoner, together with her companion; Dr. George King was drowned while escorting a party of missionaries down the Yellow River on pigskin rafts; he was attempting to refloat one of the rafts when the tragedy occurred. And Dr. Whitfield Guinness of Kaifeng, after treating Chinese soldiers, contracted typhus himself and died in Peking after being forced to take the journey there at the height of his illness.

The battle was fierce indeed. And the army of missionaries had been forced to make a tactical withdrawal. But in Shanghai, D. E. Hoste, the former artillery officer, was calmly directing operations. He was a quiet man, known for his whimsical sense of humour. But most of all he was a prayerful man and therefore a wise man— the man for the emergency. The forces at his disposal as 1927 came to an end were 1,185 missionaries and over 4,000 Chinese workers; 72,133 Chinese were in communicant membership in 1,287 organised churches. A total of over 6,000 children were receiving education in 280 C.I.M. schools while nearly 6,000 children were attending Sunday School. This was the work which, among others, the "Enemy" was attempting to destroy.

It was a dark hour. The outlook was even darker. The problems were mountainous. One half of the total force of foreign missionaries in China left the country never to return. It seemed to them and to many others that the ultimate day of trial for the Christian cause in China had come. But a C.I.M. missionary wrote, "In coming years we shall no doubt look back upon this year 1927 as one of genuine and inestimable progress for the missionary cause in this great land of China." The prophetic words were written only five days after 1,000 anti-Christian students had wrecked the chapel and cruelly beaten the elderly Chinese evangelist.

## CHAPTER II

## "ATTAQUEZ!"

"MY centre is yielding, my right is retreating; excellent situation—I am attacking!" was the message sent by Marshal Foch to Marshal Joffre at a crisis in the Battle of the Marne in 1915. Marshal Foch laid great emphasis on the value of the offensive and when his subordinate commanders threatened to fall back unless reinforced his vehement reply was always *"Attaquez! Attaquez! Attaquez!"*

The persecutions during the first three centuries of the Christian era were in the nature of enemy offensives— offensives which never succeeded in destroying the Church, though sometimes successful locally. Then, as Christians were revived again and imbued with an offensive missionary spirit, the Church, in successive waves of advance, occupied unreached areas and challenged the domination of the Usurper of Christ's Lordship in the hearts of men. This was pre-eminently the spirit of Hudson Taylor who believed that the C.I.M. must be "always advancing". Under his leadership, offensives were repeatedly launched just when the situation seemed most hopeless. A church or mission which has lost the initiative and the urge to advance, content merely to consolidate the ground already won, is certain to suffer spiritual loss.

1927 was as black a year as any for missions in China. In addition to the 5,000 foreign missionaries who left China, many others were forced to seek safety at the coast, including 800 C.I.M. missionaries. The Communists were cock-a-hoop and the anti-Christian movement reached a peak of violence with a flanking attack on the Chinese Church. Christians were denounced as traitors and "running dogs of imperialism". They suffered great indignities, persecution and even death. One Bible woman was tortured to death. Serious efforts were made here and there to suppress Christianity. Official action was taken against Christian schools which were required to register and to cease all Christian propaganda. Many Chinese intellectuals concluded that it was quite impossible to be both a patriot and a Christian. The Christian Church was undoubtedly rocked to its foundations and the world thought that it must surely collapse. Indeed it was on the verge of destruction. The situation was even more dangerous than in 1900. The Devil had wrested the offensive in an attempt to destroy Christ's Church in China. But it was abortive; he failed again. The time was ripe for the Christian movement to take the offensive.

Not that there was anything at all to encourage this. The civil war, with the increasing use of modern weapons, was becoming even more terrible. Conditions throughout the country were chaotic. After the crossing of the Yangtze in 1927 the southern forces were checked and dissension broke out. Rival Governments were set up in Peking, Nanking and Canton and there were other independent factions. The tale of human suffering caused by the war defied description. In 1928 Great Britain and the United States recognised the united Government of Chiang Kai-shek in Nanking and all restrictions on travel in the interior were removed. But banditry and lawlessness persisted. Opium was being cultivated in more provinces than at any time since 1911. The Muslim Rebellion of 1928–9 caused great loss of life and four Mission compounds were looted. Hopes of national unity were dashed in 1929 when six generals failed to agree and as from March the Central Government was engaged with the rebels. The situation seemed so hopeless that many Chinese and not a few missionaries confessed to an unprecedented depression of spirit. Typhus, too, took its toll and in that year there were more Mission deaths than in any year since 1900.

Not everyone was forced to evacuate from the interior in 1927 and 213 C.I.M. missionaries risked remaining in seventy inland stations. Many dangers frequently beset them, but they carried on their work, and even in 1927 nearly 3,000 individuals dared to confess Christ publicly in baptism. The circulation of the Scriptures reached 8 million—an astonishing figure in the circumstances.

The evacuee missionaries at the coast were not idle. Sixty-seven Japanese were won for Christ in Shanghai and golden opportunities were found among the men of the British Defence Force. But their uppermost thoughts were about the future. What were God's purposes for His Church and for the Mission? Conferences were held in several coastal centres as well as in the home countries. Serious attempts were made to grapple with the realities of the situation in China and the lessons to be learned from it. These conferences resulted in a re-affirmation of Hudson Taylor's original aim of "raising up self-supporting and self-extending churches". Decisions were reached to hasten this process by handing over the church administration to the Chinese leaders. This, it was argued, would also free the missionaries for direct evangelistic work in new areas or for special service to the Church. God, it was clear, had taken the missionaries away from their stations so that they could make a new appraisal of their work and seek fresh authority to conduct their future activities.

As the more intense anti-foreign feeling died down and the Government made friendly advances to Great Britain and the United States, missionaries began to return to their stations. There they found that the Christians had remained remarkably steadfast and were evincing a deeper faith and increased maturity: they were steadier, sturdier and wiser, less dependent and with more initiative than before. Gifts of leadership were coming to the fore and the happy relationship between the Christians and the missionaries remained unbroken. The threatening waves had beaten themselves out on the shingle. Spiritual gains outweighed the material losses. One missionary wrote, "Some of us feel that revival is near."

The people, too, were more friendly. They were readier to listen to the Gospel and to buy Christian books. In 1928 the three Bible Societies sold 11,453,783 copies of the Scriptures. It was time to advance. God was calling the Mission not merely to regain lost ground but to invade the "Enemy's" camp. D. E. Hoste was a commander after Foch's own heart. Just when the general situation was at its worst in March 1929, Hoste telegraphed to the home countries an appeal for 200 workers (the majority to be men) in the next two years. Reinforcements were desperately needed if the forward movement, based on a careful survey of the unevangelised areas of China, was to succeed. "It will involve," said the General Director, "the most tremendous conflict which we have ever undertaken as a Mission!" On the home front Brigadier-General Mackenzie, a former artillery officer who once commanded the garrison in Peking, organised the Prayer Companionship, which aimed to provide each missionary with a bodyguard of twelve praying companions. The gauntlet had been thrown down and the battle was engaged.

By the end of 1929, thirty-five of the Two Hundred were in China. Fifty-one followed in 1930 and 117 in 1931, giving a total of 203. Disappointingly, only eighty-four were men. In the providence of God the valuable old headquarters site in the Hongkew district of Shanghai was sold in 1930 and magnificent new buildings erected in another part of the Settlement with the proceeds of the sale. They were ready just in time to accommodate the large numbers of recruits in 1931 and 1932. In that year ninety-one recruits brought the total membership to 1,326. The offensive was not delayed: eighteen new stations were opened in 1929, increasing and varied evangelism led to many remarkable conversions among soldiers, opium addicts, Buddhist devotees, prisoners and even Tibetans. The most outstanding convert of 1931 was, however, the Premier himself, General Chiang Kai-shek, who was baptised into the Methodist Church; this was a bold step to take, since the Communists and many members of his own Party were still bitterly opposed to Christianity. With all his political mistakes, the Generalissimo has proved to be a sincere Christian, politically incorruptible and personally irreproachable. No other national leader in the world has been so outspokenly and unashamedly Christian in practice and in public utterance.

As if to confirm the General Director's warning, eight foreigners were murdered and thirty captured and held to ransom in the months following the call for the Two Hundred. Brigands ravaged the south-west. One band took a C.I.M. provincial superintendent captive and another was responsible for the murder of a C.I.M. missionary. In Honan five C.I.M. missionaries were held as hostages and many others were robbed or taken captive. In Kansu, famine followed in the wake of the Muslim Rebellion and George Findlay Andrew of the C.I.M. was appointed to direct the work of the International Famine Relief Organisation. For his brilliant services he was awarded the O.B.E.

But the Communists presented the greatest threat to the new offensive. Chinese Soviets had been set up in east Szechwan and in Kiangsi. Marxist propaganda strongly affected the oppressed and suffering people and but for the effect of the atrocities committed by the Red armies Communism would certainly have swept China in the 30's. Kiangsi province suffered most. Communist and bandit armies competed in outrages. A hundred and fifty thousand citizens were killed and $1\frac{1}{2}$ million fled the province. One hundred thousand homes were burnt to the ground. Twenty out of thirty-two C.I.M. stations were looted and only seven were still occupied at the time of the 1927 evacuation. In 1930 three Finnish associate missionaries were murdered and numerous Christians died as the result of Communist ill-treatment. In July 1930 a Communist army captured Changsha in Hunan and sacked the city, using the C.I.M. Bible Training Institute as their temporary headquarters.

At this point General Chiang Kai-shek determined to crush the Communists. But it was to take four years— four tragic years—before success came. Catastrophic floods, unbridled banditry and the rape of Manchuria followed in 1931—a final humiliation for the Chinese Government. China presented to the world the picture of a weak, unwieldy, disorganised country supporting huge armies which impoverished the resources of the country and completely failed to bring peace. It was a miracle that any missionary activity was possible. Only the redoubled prayers of people at home enabled the work to continue. In 1869 a member of the *Lammermuir* party had written words which were equally relevant in 1931: "Pioneering work is no child's play and Satan will not allow the prey to be taken from his grasp. In attempting to open up new places we must expect to meet with difficulties such as those only who have actually experienced them can fully comprehend."

One might have thought that an addition of 200 new workers in a time of world-wide economic distress and extensive unemployment would have excessively strained the financial resources of the Mission. But the wealth of the Mission is in God, not in investments or securities. The income actually rose from £170,499 in 1928 to £221,685 in 1929, a figure which exceeded by £36,000 any previous annual total.

In 1932 D. E. Hoste, having seen the Forward Movement well on its way appointed George Gibb of Scotland as his successor in the directorship. He had led the Mission during thirty turbulent years after the death of the founder. The new leader assumed office at a critical time, but in the true tradition he declared: "The conditions in China, in my opinion, constitute a definite challenge to go forward in the work of the Gospel. Notwithstanding the difficulties of the situation . . . the opportunities before us are simply unprecedented. Never have there been so many wide open doors for preaching the Gospel among all classes . . ."

CHAPTER 12

# REVIVAL

GOD had another answer to the defiance of Satan—
revival! The cry for revival had for long risen from the
hearts of missionaries and Chinese Christians alike.
Formality, barrenness and coldness afflicted the Church.
There was not enough fruitfulness and spiritual growth
was slow. Much hidden sin within the Church reduced
the power of her impact on the society around.

But God had been preparing His instruments to arouse
the Chinese Church. In 1926, when anti-foreign and
anti-Christian propaganda were at their height, Paget
Wilkes of the Japan Evangelistic Band held meetings in
Shanghai which kindled fires in the hearts of a number
of young Christians connected with the Bethel Mission.
Prominent among them was Andrew Gih, a post office
official. He gave up his job and formed the Bethel
Worldwide Evangelistic Band. Later Dr. John Sung, the
eccentric scientist-evangelist, joined the Band and
worked with Andrew Gih in many a powerful campaign
from Manchuria to Yunnan before breaking away to
continue his work alone. Hsieh Meng-tzi already had
long experience in revival meetings. Other names came
into prominence: Marcus Cheng, Leyland Wang, the
former naval officer, Wang Ming-tao, who was born in
the Legation Quarter in the 1900 siege, Charles Li, the
Chefoo businessman, John Li and Chia Yü-ming. Ni To-
sheng (Watchman Nee) was also well known throughout
China by his writings. This brilliant young man headed
an extensive independent church movement dubbed
"The Little Flock" which perturbed mission leaders,
but became a great spiritual force throughout China.

There were missionaries, too, with a message for the

churches: Marie Monsen of the Norwegian Mission, Anna Christensen of the C.I.M. and others. All exercised a more or less nation-wide ministry, and the message was essentially the same: the exposing of secret sin, a call to thorough repentance, the need for restitution, the sufficiency of the Blood of Christ to cleanse and deliver from all sin and the possibility of a fullness of the Holy Spirit. The results, too, were characteristic: nominal Christians were truly converted, many lives were changed, new life flooded into the churches, Christians began to witness spontaneously to others, while joy and love overflowed in Christian fellowship. "There is a new type of Christianity abroad!" said one senior missionary. Another confessed, "We feel ashamed that we have been in China for more than thirty years and did not believe that what we now see and hear was possible in this land." From all parts of China reports reached Shanghai of a transforming work of the Holy Spirit among missionaries, young and old, who began to realise that they too, as well as the Chinese Christians, needed reviving.

As in most historic revivals counterfeit movements arose, accompanied by excesses and much frothy emotionalism. One such, the "Jesus Family", with its unscriptural emphases and inconsistent conduct caused havoc in many churches. At a later date this movement, by its communal life, attempted to improve on Communism, but, in spite of some commendable features, it never quite succeeded in living down its disastrous beginnings.

The result of true revival is always a spontaneous increase in evangelism. The Bethel Bands in particular encouraged every church visited to form small voluntary preaching bands, each with its own flag and leader. Hundreds of such bands of lay witnesses became active in the wake of Bethel missions. By 1933 it was observed that the Church was growing more through self-propagation than through the work of foreign missionaries. The thorny problems of self-support, self-government and self-propagation were in fact solved only as the result of spiritual revival. Self-support was the most difficult to attain under the current economic conditions. Much progress was made in self-government in spite of natural trepidation and fear of failure. The Chinese Church began to reveal a new initiative. In Hankow a Christian daily newspaper was started. Both in Hankow and Shanghai Christian broadcasting companies operated the first wholly Christian broadcasting stations in the world. In Shansi, David Yang pioneered a unique experiment in evangelism: selected men and women studied together for six months of the year and then engaged in Christian service for six months. Young missionaries joined the team as learners. Many of the members of the "Spiritual Work Team" later became outstanding workers in different parts of China. Young Chinese in increasing numbers were planning to train for the ministry and new Bible Schools were opened to meet the need. In Szechwan the first Chinese assistant bishop, a converted Muslim, had been consecrated in 1929.

The missionaries matched the initiative of the Chinese Church. In 1933 nineteen new centres were opened in nine different provinces. Some areas of China now enjoyed more peaceful conditions than for a long time. Tent missions increased and bore much fruit. There were further attempts to enter prisons where prisoners and jailers alike were converted. Work among children and young people received greater emphasis. The student class and the intelligentsia were showing an increasing interest. Much-needed opium refuge work was undertaken. The arrival among the Two Hundred of five doctors gave medical evangelism a new impetus. Clinics based on the fourteen hospitals were used as spearheads for pioneer evangelism. The Hudson Taylor Memorial Hospital in Changsha was opened in 1936.

Both the movement among the tribes, especially the Lisu, and translation work were gathering momentum. Six members of the Two hundred, appointed to Chinese Turkestan, made an historic journey in 1932 to Urumchi (Tihwa) across Mongolia and the Gobi desert with the veteran George Hunter. Sven Hedin, the explorer, plotted their route for them. They covered 1,800 miles in twenty-two days' travelling time, much of the journey over a rough trackless desert. But they arrived safely, only to find themselves in the midst of a Muslim rebellion. Dr. Emil Fischbacher, one of the six recruits, and the veteran Percy Mather did not spare themselves in tending the wounded. Tragically, both contracted typhus and died. It was a shock to the whole community at the very commencement of the forward drive. Nevertheless three new centres were shortly opened in that remote province.

.     .     .

The number of centres from which C.I.M. missionaries were working increased by 104 between 1927 and 1936. And new methods were being tried. Visual evangelism leaped forward and attractive Gospel posters began to appear on city gates and walls. Newspaper evangelism produced results. Motor vehicles equipped with loud-speakers, projectors and screens were used for mass meetings. The people, now growing accustomed to political meetings and lectures from Communist and anti-Communist speakers, were more ready to attend missions where thoughtful lectures and addresses were given. Conversions were multiplied; professional spies, members of secret societies, opium addicts, prostitutes, gamblers, soldiers, Buddhist vegetarians, young and old, rich and poor, bandits and scholars were finding Christ.

In 1936 a record total of 8,841 baptisms was double that of 1926! This stormy decade produced altogether over 60,000 baptisms, bringing the membership of the C.I.M. churches up to 95,000.

## CHAPTER 13

# NOUGHT CAN SEPARATE

THE achievements of the preceding chapter were accomplished in the midst of China's agony: a cholera epidemic which claimed 150,000 victims, an earthquake, crop failures and the steady encroachment of Japan. In 1933 the Japanese Army landed troops near Shanghai and attacked the Chapei district. Only six weeks after the move to the new headquarters premises in Sinza Road, the original C.I.M. headquarters was destroyed by shell-fire in this attack. The Japanese further threatened Peking and Tientsin and tightened their grip on the five provinces within the bend of the Yellow River; they failed, however, in their attempt to detach them completely from the rest of China. In 1934 Henry Pu-yi, the last of the Manchu emperors, was enthroned as the puppet emperor of Manchukuo (Manchuria) by the Japanese Army. Inner Mongolia, too, was threatened. General Chiang Kai-shek was in a dilemma, for the Communists were challenging his authority internally and the Japanese threatened the country externally. Civil war rendered him too weak to oppose the greater might of Japan. The territory he effectively controlled was shrinking, so, abandoning the attempt to unify the country by force, he concentrated on achieving better government within a limited area. He launched the New Life movement, which was a recognition of the moral deterioration of the country due to misgovernment. And he personally invited the close co-operation of missions in the movement. Where there were areas of comparative peace, there was a great material progress: new roads, extended railways, efficient passenger plane services, town planning and a stabilised currency.

China was not alone in her troubles. Germany was falling into the hands of the Nazis. Abyssinia was as much a victim of blatant aggression as Manchuria. In both cases the League of Nations could do nothing but condemn these actions. War also ravaged Spain. But China's suffering was the bitterest, for the Communist armed rebellion prevented any reconstruction of the country. The struggle in Kiangsi dragged on, but throughout the entire Communist occupation, the Christians always found ways to worship, even when the chapels were being used for barracks and stables. In 1932 Ferguson, a C.I.M. missionary engaged in flood relief, was captured by the Communists who paraded him from town to town on the open-air theatre stages for the crowds to see. Ferguson used every such occasion to preach Christ fearlessly until his execution a month or two later. In the same year bandits murdered a former Chefoo schoolboy, then a missionary in Kansu. In 1933 it was the turn of Szechwan to suffer Communist depredations and Mission work was disrupted.

The following year the Central Government troops finally broke into the south Kiangsi Communist strong-hold and cleared the province. As the Communists left the churches immediately organised eighteen preaching bands, opened thirty new centres and reached out to many unevangelised villages in the province. The Bible School at Nanchang was reopened. The result was 1,100 baptisms in 1936 in Kiangsi alone, the province most cruelly ravaged under Communist rule.

The retreating Communist troops escaping to the south-west overran the station in south Anhwei where John and Betty Stam, members of the Two Hundred, were living. The Stams were caught, tried and condemned to die as imperialist spies. They contrived to hide their baby daughter and wrote their last message to a friend: "All our possessions and stores are in their hands but we praise God peace is in our hearts. The Lord bless and guide you. And as for us—may God be glorified whether by life or death." Death came to them by the sword, for they were beheaded. A Chinese friend who interceded for them died too.

The following poem was written by an anonymous composer on the death of a missionary in north China who faced his murderers unafraid. The Stams sent it home and the letter arrived on the very same day as the cable breaking the news of their martyrdom:

Afraid? Of what?
To feel the Spirit's glad release?
To pass from pain to perfect peace,
The strife and strain of life to cease?
    Afraid—of that?

Afraid? Of what?
Afraid to see the Saviour's face,
To hear His welcome and to trace
The glory gleam from wounds of grace?
    Afraid—of that?

Afraid? Of what?
A flash, a crash, a pierced heart,
Darkness, light, O Heaven's art!
A wound of His a counterpart!
    Afraid—of that?

Afraid? Of what?
To do by death what life could not—
Baptise with blood a stony plot,
Till souls shall blossom from that spot.
    Afraid—of that?

Miraculously, the Stam's infant daughter escaped death and was rescued by loving Chinese Christians.*

The same autumn the Bosshardts, the Haymans and Grace Emblen were captured in Kweichow and held for ransom by a Communist army: the ladies were soon released but Hayman spent 413 days in Communist hands with Bosshardt before he was freed. They were repeatedly threatened with death but bore a consistent testimony for Jesus Christ the whole time. As Hayman reluctantly said good-bye to his companion, Bosshardt

* *The Triumph of John and Betty Stam*, by Mrs. Howard Taylor.

said, "Pray that I may recklessly preach Jesus Christ!" Bosshardt remained in Communist hands for a further 147 days before his release in the vicinity of Kunming.

Harried by Government troops and threatened with extinction the Communist armies in 1935 made their escape through Szechwan and the Tibetan marches north to Yenan in Shensi. Their "Long March" is an epic story. *En route* they pillaged and killed: Tibetan lamas or Chinese peasants, it mattered little. Alarm heralded their approach. Mission stations were speedily evacuated, looted and then re-occupied as the army passed on. Early in the year, a party of seventy Chefoo schoolchildren and their escort were returning to Chefoo by sea when their vessel, the S.S. *Tungchow* was boarded by pirates and held for two tense days before its release. Nowhere seemed safe. The same year Sinkiang (Turkestan) came under Russian control. Miss Cable and the Misses French were arrested and held for months by a Communist army. Mildred Cable wrote: 'We are in a satanic whirlwind".

The general situation was so bad that in 1935, none but men (with three special exceptions) were allowed to sail from the home countries. The climax came in December 1936 when General Chiang Kai-shek went in person to Sian to deal with an uprising of disaffected troops. There he was kidnapped by pro-Communist troops and held prisoner for two weeks. The country held its breath. When asked by his captors what he required he said "A Bible only!" and this he was given. During his captivity Chiang agreed with the Communists to adopt a tougher attitude towards the Japanese. This settled, the Generalissimo was released on Christmas Day to the great joy of the nation. Early in 1937 the Communist armies deliberately provoked the Japanese by crossing the Yellow River into Shansi, a Japanese "sphere of influence". The Shansi invasion disrupted missionary work in the whole province. City after city where C.I.M. missionaries were living was besieged and there was grave danger to life until the Communists withdrew.

The 30's were notorious for world-wide economic

depression. Conditions in North America became critical in 1933 when many banks were closed and thousands of citizens ruined. Inevitably Mission donors suffered. Nevertheless, the C.I.M. continued to advance! A time of want, of chastening and of testing was also a period of miraculous provision. In 1932 600 new donors were added in Great Britain and 400 in North America. The overall increase of £10,000 was most timely in a year which saw the arrival of ninety-one recruits in China. Ninety more followed in 1934 to bring the membership of the Mission to the highest peak in its history—1,368. The next year the income rose to £159,252, the largest total since 1929. It was with wonder and thanksgiving that members of the Mission proved again that they could leave all the responsibility for the work and its maintenance with God.

In January 1937 Frank Houghton, for many years the British Editorial Secretary, was consecrated Bishop of the C.I.M. section of the west China diocese.

The year opened auspiciously. For the first time for many years there was no active civil war. The Communists were comparatively quiet in their north Shensi base. But Japanese pressure was increasing. In July, as Chinese and Japanese troops were holding military exercises outside Peking near the Marco Polo Bridge, a shot was fired. A Japanese soldier fell. And the Sino-Japanese War of 1937–45 began. That shot reverberated around the world and prefaced the Second World War of 1939–45. The sound of crashing bombs and bursting shells nearly drowned the voice of the Church. Only medical workers received permission to return from furlough. They were direly needed. By the end of the year most of the provinces were affected by war, although it seriously dislocated missionary work only in the coastal provinces. Everybody was now asking, "What new and strange purposes has God now?"

## CHAPTER 14

# DANGEROUS OPPORTUNITY

In all the 4,000 years of China's history, the war with Japan was her most critical period. The Chinese word for crisis can be translated literally as "dangerous opportunity". Beset by every imaginable danger for eight years, the Church and the missionary body certainly found these war years to be years of extraordinary and unprecedented opportunities.

To reach China entailed dangers enough. C.I.M. missionaries were torpedoed, bombed from the air at sea and had miraculous escapes from death. Once in China, they faced the perils of aerial bombing, fierce battles for key cities, military occupation, cholera, typhus, flood and famine. Altogether over ten missionaries of the Mission lost their lives in plane crashes, road accidents, typhus epidemics, air-raids and the like. This number included two superintendents and Rowland Hogben the British Men Candidates Secretary who died in an accident on the Burma Road as he was just beginning a tour of the field. The brutal and relentless invasion of China by Japan caused unparalleled suffering to the people of China; the destruction, sorrow and mental suffering and death can never be estimated. C.I.M. missionaries, it was agreed, should remain at their posts as long as possible. It was in sharing in China's sufferings and fulfilling a Christ-like ministry to the sufferers that the missionary movement gained a new status and respect among all classes of people. The hands of the clock were pointing to the hour for action and the golden opportunity for which the Church had waited for so long had arrived.

Early in 1938 the war swept through Shantung,

Hopeh and Shansi. Much of Shanghai outside the Settlements was reduced to ruins. Nanking was engulfed; Hsuchow, Kaifeng, Anking, Hankow, Canton soon followed. The suffering of the civilian population beggars description. Half the C.I.M. stations were within the area of fighting. Missionaries at once began to care for the refugees, many of whom sought refuge in the safety of mission compounds from the cruel and vicious Japanese soldiery. This was an opportunity to care for the wounded, shelter the fearful, feed the destitute, comfort the dying and bereaved, befriend the orphans and make Christ known to all.

The catastrophic floods in Hopeh in 1939, covering one-third of the province, gave scope for flood relief in the badly-affected city of Tientsin where 24,000 refugees were in desperate need; Dr. Stanley Hoyte was put in charge of a temporary hospital. When the Chinese Army deliberately broke the dykes of the Yellow River as a defence measure against the invaders, hundreds of thousands were rendered homeless in Honan: there too C.I.M. missionaries helped in the organisation of welfare camps. In Shanghai, the most congested city in the world, members of the Mission worked with the International Relief Association in some of the 148 camps where more than 132,000 refugees were cared for and rehabilitated. In Nanking another member of the Mission found a wonderful field among the 70,000 opium addicts in that city alone. A profound impression was made on the people of China by the practical sympathy of all missionaries, and this did more than anything else to convince them of the reality of the power of Christ.

The Japanese invasion set in motion the greatest migration of population in modern times. Homes and shops in the threatened areas were abandoned and carrying only a few possessions people set off on the long trek to the West to escape the terror of Japanese occupation. The trickle became a flood and it is estimated that eventually from 40 to 60 million people were involved. The refugees were strafed from the air, suffered shortage of food and became ill with cholera and typhoid.

Children were separated from their parents, the younger members of the family from the old, many of whom were left behind to care for the ancestral home in Occupied China. There in Free China, men and women of every province found themselves rubbing shoulders with the more backward and conservative folk of the West. Every Chinese dialect was heard and English frequently became a common medium of conversation among the educated. The Central Government transferred its capital from Nanking to Chungking. But even there, whenever the cover of clouds permitted, the people knew they could expect wave after wave of Japanese bombers raining death and destruction. The old city was destroyed, but the Government proceeded at once to rebuild it on modern lines. Chungking became the symbol of resistance against the common enemy.

The Church in the Occupied eastern provinces was larger and more firmly-established than that in the west, and therefore better equipped to meet the severe onslaught. But it still desperately needed the help of the missionaries. A return to the Hopeh stations was possible in 1938, though the situation was precarious and fraught with physical danger. Japanese armies, puppet Chinese armies, Nationalist armies and Communist armies were all on the march throughout the countryside. Yet the only Christian deaths were at the hands of bandits. The missionaries found that the faith of the believers had been strengthened through their recent sufferings. One woman testified: "During this past year my home has been twice burnt and nothing has been saved. Four out of six relatives there have died, including my brother who was branded with a hot iron. My daughter-in-law was shot through the lungs before my eyes and my only little grandson died of exposure. Yet I will not let go of Jesus Christ. I will not blame Him!" Stories like this were common. Christians learned to sing, "Who shall separate us from the love of Christ? Shall tribulation, or distress, or persecution, or famine, or nakedness, or peril, or sword? Nay, in all these things we are more than conquerors through Him that loved us."

Far from being discouraged by their sufferings and losses, the Christians rebuilt their chapels, re-doubled their evangelistic activity and demonstrated that their faith had only been strengthened as the result of the trials of the Church. They showed extraordinary powers of recuperation and in a constantly-changing situation the Church came to be recognised by all as the only unchanging factor. New interest was evinced in the Gospel and the sale of Scriptures reached new records. When Christians had to flee, the one possession they could not leave behind was their Bible. A remote church in the mountains of west Shansi, which was captured and re-captured repeatedly, sent in a regular order every ten days to the Religious Tract Society in Hankow for Scriptures and Bibles to keep its bookshop supplied.

The general situation, if not impossible, was outwardly most unfavourable for missionary work. Yet when the Home Directors met in Shanghai in 1938 all their plans were for advance. With faith deeply rooted in the purposes and promises of God, the Conference re-affirmed that God's commission to the Mission had not been revoked and that the work must go on. Every aspect of the work was carefully considered. Past mistakes were recognised. The necessary adjustments were honestly faced. New recruits of the highest calibre would be welcomed. Assistant Regional directors were appointed for the first time to lessen the burden of the administration resting on the shoulders of the General Director. The Conference was described as marking the opening of a new era in the history of the Mission. Although some recruits were soon on their way, the training of women recruits was later suspended because of the war situation and only one recruit reached China during the last three war years.

Conditions in Occupied China were forcing as many missionaries as possible to make their way from Occupied China to Free China. Access to the interior became increasingly difficult; circuitous and dangerous journeys were often made in order to reach destinations in the west. Some travelled via Haiphong and the Yunnan railway, others via Singapore, Rangoon and the Burma

Road. This was an experience which none who made the journey can ever forget: 600 miles of spectacular road, winding and crawling over lofty and majestic mountain ranges or snaking down to the deep gorges of the Salween and Mekong: driving hazards, breakdowns ("casting anchor"), hitchhikers ("yellow fish"), tropical storms, long delays, flooded rivers, doubtful inns, air-raid alarms, all made each traveller's experience a kaleidoscope of excitement.

The Shanghai headquarters of the Mission made every effort to maintain contact with the 329 stations in Occupied and in Free China. News received daily covered the whole gamut of emotion: tragedy, comedy, joy and sorrow, fear and faith, peace and alarm. In 1939 the incomplete figure of baptisms was a record—9,364: the total number for the year may well have exceeded 10,000. In Hunan, the long-resistant province, over 1,000 people confessed Christ in baptism in C.I.M. churches alone.

The miracle of finance was no less amazing. The favourable rate of exchange swelled the value of the income in 1938 to meet the increased expenditure. In 1939 income increased by £10,000. This, with the fall in exchange rate, produced the largest income in terms of Chinese dollars in the history of the Mission. But the soaring prices and the alarming increase in the cost of living required increasing austerity. In 1939 Great Britain declared war on Germany, but even the vicissitudes of the long conflict did not invalidate the principle of implicit trust in God.

George Gibb resigned the General Directorship of the Mission in favour of Bishop Frank Houghton in 1940. He died soon after. During May of that year the headquarters of the Mission in London was seriously damaged by enemy action in a fierce air attack on London. Despite the "blitz", 800 people attended the Annual Meeting in the Queens Hall three days later.

The situation in the Pacific became so threatening in October that the Mission set up an emergency headquarters in Chungking. Two of the Regional Directors and the Treasurer moved first, to be joined by Bishop

Houghton in February 1941. But for this God-guided arrangement the Mission would have suffered a staggering blow when the attack on Pearl Harbour occurred on December 7th. The Settlement in Shanghai was then taken over by the Japanese Army and all bank deposits frozen. Five thousand pounds which should have been sent to Shanghai in November was providentially delayed until after December 7th and became available when the new headquarters began to function in Chungking. Sufficient funds remained in Shanghai for immediate use. At the time of Pearl Harbour there were 950 missionaries on the field: 250 in Occupied China and 700 in Free China. But in spite of war conditions in Europe, of high taxation and the restrictions on the amount of money permitted to be sent to China from Britain, it must be recorded to the glory of God that the income from Great Britain did not diminish: indeed, it even increased by £8,000 in 1941. The "pegging" of the rate of exchange by the Chinese Government to a totally unrealistic figure drastically reduced the purchasing power of the pound and the dollar and caused acute hardship to all missionaries. In God's over-ruling providence the larger contribution to the Mission's funds came from North America in most of the war years.

No immediate action was taken after Pearl Harbour to intern British and American nationals, though Patrick Bruce, Headmaster of the Chefoo School, was arrested and held for six weeks. When the schoolchildren and staff were eventually moved out of their buildings under Japanese armed escort, they marched off to the singing of:

> God is still on the throne,
> And He will remember His own;
> His promise is true,
> He will not forget you;
> God is still on the throne.

In their new premises on Temple Hill seventy-one girls and staff were crowded into a house built for a family of six. The boys were similarly crowded. It was therefore a relief when in September 1943 all were moved to a large civilian internment camp at Weihsien. There in a community of 1,800 the children were thrown together with all sorts and conditions of men but soon established a reputation as the "finest bunch of boys and girls ever met!" In Shanghai the missionaries of the C.I.M. were distributed among two camps in Shanghai and Yangchow, where bishops and burglars, ladies and prostitutes, missionaries and merchants lived together for nearly three years of privation, squalor, uncertainty and hope that never died. As for the German members of the Mission, the tables were turned in comparison with the First World War. This time it was their turn to minister in practical ways to their British and American brethren in Christ. The C.I.M. headquarters building at first became a training centre for Japanese recruits and then the Japanese Army H.Q. The Mission now found itself in two halves sealed off from each other for the duration of the war. Missionaries of neutral nations were able to continue their work under Japanese government in a limited way, but the chief interest centred in west China.

"Our main concern," wrote a Director, "is with the advance of the Gospel in China. Our commission is founded upon the purpose of God. Our God is not daunted because of opposition. Amid the confusion of war and the upheaval of society in China, His purpose stands. All that is merely man's work is being removed, but amid the destruction He is also doing 'new things'. We face great and increasing difficulties but God is our sufficiency. This glad fact seized and held with the daring of faith destroys pessimism and provides a greater driving force than any so-called optimism."

The face of west China was completely transformed by the great migration. Communications were vastly improved to cope with the war traffic. Trucks could now travel from Kunming to Chungking in eight days instead of forty by the old means of transport. The Burma Road was extended many thousands of miles to Kansu and Sinkiang, and another highway carried traffic from

Yunnan right up to the Tibetan border. Air services were frequent and efficient. After 1942, when China's road link with the outside world through Burma was severed, alcohol and charcoal trucks lumbered slowly along the highways and petrol was a precious commodity. But the traffic kept moving. Government offices, universities and other educational institutions sprawled widely over eleven provinces of Free China. There were ten universities in Yunnan, ten in Szechwan and six in Kweichow.

But the backwoods people of the west and the more cultured people of the east found it difficult to meet and to mingle freely; language difficulties were great, but the greatest problem was that the sophisticated easterners tended to despise their backward, unhygienic and conservative fellow-countrymen of the west. This attitude was reflected in the churches where the progressive and active Christians from "down-river" were given a very lukewarm reception by the often timid and apathetic local Christians. The Church in the west was quite incapable of meeting the new situation. The local Christians were seeing for the first time in their own countrymen examples of what Christians could and ought to be. Some Christians from the coastal areas immigrated in communities and became ready-made churches, eager to witness in church-less areas.

Moreover, in recent years Chinese leaders had been emerging full of faith and the Holy Spirit. Mighty in the Scriptures, they found a welcome throughout Free China: James Tien of Mukden, Peter Yen of Shansi, Marcus Cheng of Changsha, Calvin Chao of Nanking, Andrew Gih of Shanghai, and others infused new life into moribund churches. Many a church experienced a kind of resurrection. New churches on the ashes of the old grew up in the Kweichow capital and in its second city of Anshun. Kweiyang, instead of being the place where corrupt officials garnered their opium profits, became one of the most important centres in Free China where university and Government institutions, the Red Cross and high schools contributed to the doubling of the population. Anshun, too, harboured military academies and agricultural stations. Naturally the field was no longer a C.I.M. monopoly, for refugee missionaries and organisations kept arriving and new churches sprang into existence. English services became a popular attraction for the more cultured; many students, doctors and nurses through attending English Bible classes found Christ there. There were large sales of the Scriptures and the Bible Society could not cope adequately with the demand. Only the local populace remained to a large extent unresponsive, though even among them there were outstanding conversions. Never had there been such opportunities in west China. They were exciting if exhausting and exacting years.

## CHAPTER 15

# LIKE A MIGHTY ARMY

THE C.I.M. is an interdenominational fellowship. It is decidedly not undenominational. Each member retains a loyalty to his own denomination or church from which he is sent out and by which he is supported. But it has not been the aim of the Mission merely to reproduce Western denominations in China. The hope was to plant churches which would be truly indigenous and not exotic: fully Chinese churches, under Chinese leadership, supported by Chinese money and independent of Western control. In this the Mission did not always succeed and often fell into the snare common to all Mission organisations of trying to exercise too much control over the churches they founded. But the transplanting of Western denominations—extensions of one or other of the multiplicity of large and small denominations—in a foreign soil has been belatedly recognised by Church leaders as a major error. The Communists now denounce the introduction of denominational distinctions into China as an imperialist plot to retain foreign control of the churches. The Church in China today has been left the task of demonstrating that Christianity is not merely the white man's religion, tied to European plans for national aggrandisement. The C.I.M. possibly saw this principle at an earlier date than most and was the first to make serious attempts to promote "the three autonomies" in 1928. The war gave fresh urgency to the full achievement of complete independence for the churches.

Frequent conferences in Free China between missionaries and church leaders were concerned with the practical problems involved. Mutual confidence increased as the churches were convinced that the Mission's desire to give every possible aid to full autonomy was genuine. In Honan, where four-fifths of the province was in Free China, a Japanese offensive in 1941 drove many from their homes. Though chapels and mission premises were bombed, looted and burned, the Church maintained all its activities and began to employ its own pastors. In 1943 floods and crop failures caused a terrible famine, and when a snow blizzard overtook the emaciated sufferers the following winter, 2,000 corpses were collected on the streets of one city alone. Then in May the Yellow River dykes burst and 400,000 more were rendered homeless. Relapsing fever, a plague of locusts and another Japanese invasion increased the general misery. But in the face of every disaster the Church never wavered and the sympathetic generosity of Christians in other provinces deepened the consciousness of Christian unity and fellowship.

The churches in Anhwei shouldered their responsibilities with courage and efficiency. The first twenty-five years of work in that field had been laboriously slow and discouraging, producing only five city groups and six out-stations—a feeble company. But during the second twenty-five years the city churches increased to forty, and country churches to sixty. Fowyang was in fact the hub of 100 churches. This spectacular progress was the fruit of a vigorous programme of evangelism and Bible teaching which strongly emphasised the duty of tithing. In 1943 several pastors were ordained and the generosity of the Christians increased. In the following year the eight district unions of Fowyang united to form a county union. Thus when the missionaries left in 1945 the Church was poised to advance.

In June 1942, after two months of incessant bombing, the Japanese advanced deeper into Kiangsi with the aim of destroying the new railway and plundering for food and raw materials. Missionary premises in five towns were looted and then burned to the ground. Many of the older Christians who could not escape lost their lives. Five city churches which had once been centres of spiritual life and witness were reduced to charred ruins.

The heathen taunted the Christians but the faith of most remained strong. In one town where nine-tenths of the buildings were destroyed 500 Christians went on meeting for worship in one of the damaged buildings, the church growing spontaneously. Progress towards a healthy independence continued in several centres.

In neighbouring Chekiang the Provincial Church Council assumed full responsibility for the property and the administration of the churches and agreed to plan and support the work of the missionaries. Wenchow, Pingyang, and Wenling were encouragingly independent. Wenling had fifty-three country churches, many with imposing chapels. Missionaries were welcomed as advisors.

The north-west provinces had been suddenly brought to life by the influx of factories, the development of oil wells, the advent of Government offices and educational institutions of all kinds. For centuries an endless stream of traffic had followed the ancient Silk Road from Sian to Lanchow and over the Gobi Desert to Central Asia, but never until recently had there been motor-buses, motor-trucks and planes flying overhead. Even a railway was under construction. Suchow, Lanchow and Tienshui were the most affected cities. The local churches were weak in leadership and barely holding on when the refugees began to stream in, bringing new life and energy to the Christian cause. The "Jesus Family" caused more harm in this area than anywhere else in China. Their obsession with physical and psychical phenomena, (loud praying, shaking and hysteria), a bitter anti-foreign spirit and frequent outspoken abuse of missionaries had split the churches in several places. It was, therefore, a great day when in 1944 seventy old-established churches representing the fruit of the work of three Missions united to form a single church federation.

In the south-west encouraging developments were taking place along the Burma Road to Kunming. C.I.M. chapel services were swelled by "down-river" Christians who tended to oust the local Christians from positions of leadership: university professors, postmasters and others became active in the work of the churches. The church at Anshun developed so well that it invited its own pastor and the missionaries were able to move away to another assignment.

.    .    .

In October 1943 Chungking was the meeting-place of the China Council of the C.I.M. for what was to prove an historic session. The centrality of the Church in the purposes of God was the theme under discussion. No one knew when the war might come to an end, but together the members of the Council consulted on the policies to be adopted after the war. It was finally agreed that the Mission would offer its services as an auxiliary agency to the Church; its members would serve within the local churches in a co-operative capacity and under the local church leadership. This decision was a significant step forward in the relation of church and mission.

But the end of the war was not yet in sight. Much still remained to be done in Free China. Medical work found a boundless scope. Paoshan was chosen as the site of a new hospital to be staffed largely from the evacuated members of the Kaifeng Hospital. When suitable premises could not be found there, historic and beautiful Tali with its three ancient seventh-century pagodas was chosen instead. Some months later the hospital staff recognised the guiding hand of God when a heavy air-raid razed Paoshan to the ground. In Szechwan mobile medical evangelism was very fruitful. In Lanchow, the Kansu capital, the leprosarium continued to witness to Chinese, Muslims, Tibetans and tribal people. A new clinic in the city met the needs of others. Cholera, plague, typhus, malignant and relapsing fever were among the epidemic diseases which the medical staff had to combat. The universal lack of drugs and some-times of hospital personnel were among the handicaps under which all nineteen C.I.M. doctors worked. Their services were recognised by the Government in a statement which said: "All have courageously stood by their posts and done their best to meet the medical needs in the war areas."

## CHAPTER 16

# NOT MANY MIGHTY

WHEN Bishop Houghton first reached Chungking he was visited by five "red-hot" Christian men in the Government pleading for some young C.I.M. missionaries to devote their whole time to work among civil servants and students. They promised to provide all that might be necessary in their work. "This," they asserted, "is one of the greatest days for God's work in China!" The example of the President and other Christians, the effect of the upheaval from their traditional environment and the search for true satisfaction, all contributed to the prevailing openness of mind to the Christian Gospel among China's *élite*. More officials than ever before were reading the Bible. Three out of the seven members of the People's Political Council were Christians, one of them a woman. One high official urged, "Now is the glorious opportunity of preaching the Gospel: let us do all we can!" A Christian University Professor from Peking said, "All their hopes and helps have failed and so they have come to us!" China was at a crossroads and would never be the same again. The way the opportunity was treated might alter the whole future of China. In Chungking Bible classes were held in the homes of numerous Government servants. Their wives organised prayer-meetings and fellowship groups for their friends, at which missionaries were frequently invited to speak. Said one man, "I am not a Christian, but I believe our country will never prosper unless our people have faith in God. After the war I predict a very great advance for Christianity in China."

Mr. Ernest Yin of the Ministry of Finance was a mature and zealous Christian. In 1942 he founded the

Holy Light School for the children of people in Government circles. He invited qualified C.I.M. missionaries to serve on the staff. In 1942 there were 280 boys and girls in the school, many of them from the most senior Government families. Some became Christians and have made an outstanding contribution to the Christian Church in China and elsewhere. The school, situated in a district where there were many colleges and homes of Government officials, also became a centre for regular worship and for conferences. Generals, provincial governors and other dignitaries often worshipped there.

By order of the Department of Education, all universities began to move west in 1938 as the Japanese armies advanced. Even the libraries accompanied the colleges. One university was bombed out of eight places as it moved from one town to another. Some students walked for ninety days to reach their destination. These refugee students excited the greatest sympathy and admiration. To the local people their outlandish dress made them look like foreigners. They had come from the comforts and even the luxuries of the great cities now in the hands of the Japanese to the bare temples and crude accommodation of the west. With their professors they constituted the cream of Chinese culture. Besides the universities, research establishments, military academies, air training schools and motor mechanic schools found their way to Free China, sometimes to the most inaccessible places. In Kunming, where the population increased by 1 million in the first six months of 1938, the South West Union University, consisting of three previously separate universities, at once became a mission field for Paul and Maida Contento. An open home, a taste of forgotten comfort and the study of the Bible in English drew the students. These once proud, anti-Christian young people had become friendly almost overnight, and now attended with an inquiring mind to Christianity. Missionaries and Chinese preachers were actually welcomed on to university campuses while professors openly organised student Christian groups. Students and professors attended English services in large numbers and even associated with the backward, rather unfriendly local Christians in their simple churches. For many of these "down-river" students this was their first acquaintance with vital Christianity and they liked what they saw. There had never before been such an opportunity to reach the intelligentsia of China. C.I.M. missionaries in twenty cities devoted themselves in whole or in part to reaching students. Many were truly converted and became fervent witnesses for Christ. Two hundred were baptised in Kunming alone. This was the beginning of a movement which was to grow surprisingly after the war. Realising that it was harder to become a Christian in the agnostic and even atheistic atmosphere of the university than at high school, missionaries also pressed forward with work among high school students, many of whom were hundreds of miles from their parents and home and so open to every kind of temptation. Camps, Vacation Bible Schools and Bible classes attracted them, too.

Fourteen years earlier Calvin Chao, a Christian graduate had begun to pray that God would visit the universities of China. Now he saw the answer to his prayers. Under the inspiration of his leadership 168 delegates from many universities and colleges met for a conference on the hills outside Chungking in August 1945. Most were recent converts and each represented the miracle of a transformed life. They agreed to start a permanent student organisation. A constitution was drawn up. A Standing Committee of seven students and seven senior advisers, one of whom was a C.I.M. missionary, was elected. A monthly bulletin was to be published. At the end of the Conference eighty responded to a call to full-time service for Christ. The Conference revealed that a spirit of true revival was abroad in the universities, and that there had been hundreds of thorough-going conversions. The Bible was loved and prayer was given a large place: in one university in Shensi, thirty students used to rise at dawn every morning to pray together on a hillside.

But the war dragged on. The economic situation became more and more desperate. Catastrophic inflation set in. There were severe food shortages, in which missionary children suffered most. Many missionaries were battle-weary. There was no one to relieve them and visits to holiday resorts were impossible. Only a very few furloughs could be granted. The wonder was that the Mission survived. China was the most expensive place in the world to live. Yet God had His way of supplying material needs. There was an astonishing increase in contributions from all the home countries; it was possible to sell non-essential missionary belongings at luxury prices and Chinese Christian friends gave generously. When the situation was at its worst God intervened. In 1944 the purchasing power of the pound and the dollar fell so low that the united missionary societies appealed urgently to the authorities. In answer to prayer the Government agreed to quadruple the previous rate of exchange. This relief came in the nick of time!

In other ways, too, 1944 proved to be one of the most difficult years the Mission had ever had to face. Eight members of the Mission lost their lives, three of them in a plane crash. The year which began promisingly enough ended in disaster. First the Japanese drive in the spring forced the evacuation of all missionaries from Honan, Anhwei and Kiangsi. Then in the autumn the Japanese Army drove on through Hunan to threaten the Kweichow capital and the Burma Road. Chungking itself was thus in danger. In Chungking a Chinese Team of Witness drawn from various denominations had been very active in various forms of city-wide evangelism. As the new crisis loomed up, this group called the Christians of Free China to three days of prayer and fasting. They notified the President of their action. Almost miraculously, the Japanese drive on Kweiyang was halted amid the early snows of winter. The Burma Road was not reached and the threat was never repeated. The President later publicly acknowledged the place that prayer had played in stemming the Japanese advance.

In December the British Embassy, fearing the worst, advised the evacuation to India of all non-essential personnel. John Sinton, the Acting Field Director, in the absence of the General Director on sick leave, was faced with a very difficult decision. He ordered the evacuation. The Chefoo School children were among the first to leave for their new school in Kalimpong. Scores of other C.I.M. missionaries followed, flying "over the hump" from Chungking to Calcutta via Kunming. This is a bare statement. For the journey was by no means easy. The plane flying the children from Chungking to Kunming could not land because of an alert at the airfield: after circling round it finally made a safe landing at an emergency airfield with an empty petrol tank! Though many military planes had been lost in the extreme turbulence over the Himalayas, all the evacuee flights were safely completed. India provided a pleasant interlude for those awaiting shipping to take them back to Great Britain or the United States. The few who did not leave China were redesignated to the north-west. But by the end of the year all China except the north-west, Szechwan and Yunnan was devoid of missionaries. In east China only neutral associate missionaries remained.

December 1944 was a dark month for the nation, possibly the darkest moment in all her long history. After seven and a half years of war the whole country was wrapped in gloom. Defeat seemed inevitable. But then the Japanese tide of success began to ebb and by the end of the next year it was to be all over. First the Germans were defeated in Europe. May 8th was V.E. Day. The desperate Japanese drive towards India had been blunted and flung back, and the mainland of Japan was experiencing long-range bombing. Then Burma was recovered and the land route to China re-opened. On July 26th, 1945 Japan was offered the Potsdam terms of surrender. Receiving no answer the Americans dropped the atomic bomb on Hiroshima on August 5th. Three days later Russia declared war on Japan and invaded Manchuria. "Emperor" Henry Pu-yi became a prisoner of the Russians. (After his release he became a gardener in Peking, the city where he had once ruled an empire!) A second demand to

Japan to surrender was also rejected and the second atomic bomb fell on Nagasaki. Japan surrendered. The long war was over.

In China the Communist guerrilla forces were in the best strategic position to take the surrender of the Japanese forces and they were quick to do so. Chefoo was seized. The Nationalist China Army hastened to key cities in the east and Manchuria with the aid of American transport planes, but the Communists had already seized their opportunity and were poised to continue their struggle for victory.

At Weihsien the internees had kept in touch with world events by a secret radio. But when on August 17th the sky over the camp filled with green, cream and gold umbrellas falling from a B.29 the joy of the 200 children as well as the adults, knew no bounds. One of the parachutists was an Old Chefoo boy! In Shanghai, too, the internees were released unscathed. Four hundred internees were invited by their Chinese friends to a feast. They felt themselves engulfed in an overflow of Christian love. There was a spontaneity of joy and a manifest desire for continued close fellowship in the work of the Church. The experience thrilled and satisfied the hearts of all. Soon they were on their way home for a much-needed holiday before returning to their work.

Members of the Chungking staff made their way as quickly as possible to Shanghai where the Japanese were evicted from the Mission headquarters in Sinza Road. The task of re-occupation and rehabilitation began.

## CHAPTER 17

# OF EVERY TRIBE

THE war was over. Japan was defeated. But soon the civil war flared up again. The Communists achieved major successes in Manchuria. They already occupied much of north China. The prospects for the Central Government were dim. The economy was in a parlous condition. Inefficiency and corruption produced dangerous inflation. And inflation inevitably breeds lawlessness: of this there was plenty all over China. The morale of the people, following hard on the relief of victory over Japan, slumped to an alarming extent. The long-term prospects for missionary work in China were gloomy. The situation was not yet impossible, but it was certainly forbidding. Nothing deterred, missionaries poured back to China prepared to face whatever difficulties there might be.

The entire passenger list of the S.S. *Marine Lynx*, a former U.S. military transport ship, consisted of missionaries when she sailed from the Golden Gate for Shanghai in December 1946. The women and children were in one hold sleeping in four-tier canvas berths, while the men were in another hold. Christmas on board was unusual and anything in the nature of a pleasure cruise was lacking. All was forgotten in the joy of return to China in January 1947. With the least possible delay the 300 passengers made their way to stations all over China and the *Marine Lynx* returned for more. The great trek back to China was well under way.

. . .

Post-war surveys assure us that there are up to 2,000 tribes in the world without a Bible-rooted church and, therefore, without a strong church. The task of reaching these often remote and inaccessible people demand, missionaries of pioneer calibre. Up to 150 of these tribes are to be found in the great mountain massif of south-west China, Burma, Thailand, Vietnam and Laos—whither they have been slowly forced by the pressure of Chinese might to retreat from the wide plains of China where they once lived in comfort and prosperity. There may be as many as 15 million tribespeople in China alone.

Many thrilling tales of pioneer hardship endured by those engaged in the remarkable work among the tribes have yet to be told. Beginning at Anshun in Kweichow, the movement spread into Yunnan and across the Burma border, soon affecting half a dozen other tribes. Strong and large churches developed among the Lisu, the Nosu, the Lahu and the Miao (Meo). This chapter gathers up the threads of the story and summarises the history of the evangelisation of China's tribal minorities.

J. O. Fraser, the engineer-musician who arrived in Yunnan in 1910 at the age of twenty-two, immediately fell in love with the Lisu tribe, which opened its heart to him. It was the year of Halley's comet. But it was also the year when "God struck a match and the Lisu forest burst into flames. The wind swept the fire nine days' journey to the north." The initial spreading of our "Good News" was surprisingly rapid. Fraser invented his own "Fraser Script" and gave himself to the translation of Scripture portions into Lisu. The New Testament was completed in 1938.

When the Allens and the Cookes took up the work of translation, Fraser increasingly gave his time to a teaching and pastoral ministry. In 1916, and only after long travail and toil and prayer, did the real break-through come. The Lisu began to turn from their demon worship to Christ in large numbers and the task of teaching, catechising and shepherding the new believers and building up the young churches was overwhelming. Lisu missionaries alone were instrumental in leading 700 families of their fellow tribesmen into the Christian faith in 1918, bringing the total of baptisms since the beginning up to 60,000. Great emphasis was laid on regular Bible teaching. The Rainy Season Bible School became a regular event. The Christians gradually became literate and developed considerable gifts and ability. Leadership flowered. John Kuhn went to Lisuland in 1928. J. O. Fraser married in 1929. But nine years later, at the height of his powers and with a wealth of experience, Fraser contracted malignant malaria while on a trip in the mountains and died. He had well earned the right to be called the "apostle to the Lisu". John Kuhn accepted the torch of leadership from Fraser while Isobel Kuhn, through her books, attracted world-wide attention to the movement among the Lisu. In 1943 the Lisu Church was organised on an entirely autonomous basis. Each church had its own elected deacons and from these the Central Church Council was chosen to govern the whole district. A Lisu gospel magazine first appeared in 1944.

.     .     .

Another tribe, the Nosu, is scattered across the north of Yunnan, through Kweichow and links up with the Independent Nosu of Sikang near the Tibetan border. They are physically stronger and healthier than the Lisu but the Church was never quite as strong. The Nosu New Testament was completed in 1941 but because of war conditions it did not become available to the Church until 1949. The centre of the thirty Nosu churches was Salowu, where a chapel to seat 1,000 was built and where a permanent Bible School was situated. Two short-term Bible Schools for the sixty elders, deacons and preachers were also held annually. The Christians were liberal in their giving and achieved the ideal of the "three autonomies" much earlier than even the Chinese churches in the province. In 1937 a revival in the Bible School was marked by spontaneous confession of sin. It was in a time of snow but the fire of God fell. That year seventy-two new families were added to the Church and ninety-four more the following year. Two years later a spirit of prayer was poured out on the tribal Christians both at Salowu (Nosu) and at Sapushan (Lisu); in the following March during the United Tribes Bible School at Salowu, a spirit of revival affected the whole community. Lives were transformed and joy abounded. This was no mere burst of emotion, because the effect was lasting and the movement spread. In 1940 special meetings held by Chang Chi-cheng of the Kunming Bible School and Dan Smith led to a fresh outburst of evangelistic fervour: a large band of young people went out into lawless country to preach the Gospel and won 117 families for Christ. Two men responded to a call of God to do pioneer work among their Independent Nosu relatives of Sikang. The blessing overflowed to the Miao (Meo) of north Yunnan for whom 1940 became a red-letter year. Dr. John Sung's meetings in Kunming also kindled a fire in many hearts. Prayer, fasting and generous gifts for evangelism were among the results. Eighty were baptised in the autumn and 500 met around the Communion Table.

About this time an entry was gained into the Kachin tribe, notorious for its drunkenness and lawlessness—an unlikely seed plot for the Gospel, but one which was to produce a rich harvest.

. . . .

Good progress continued in Kweichow where the tribal work began. Dr. Fish was the first medical superintendent of a new hospital for the tribes in Anshun, opened in 1915. Most of the Kweichow tribes were branches of the Miao tribe. The transforming effect on their way of life was so remarkable that 1,000 Chinese families destroyed their idols and became Christians. During the course of one journey through the wild Kweichow mountains, Fish saw over 1,200 patients and Adam baptised 194 men and women from five different tribes. The sudden death of Adam when he was struck by lightning in his own home, superstitiously looked on as a judgment from God, was a serious setback to the work, until in 1935 God used a young Welshman, Ieuan Jones, to bring fresh streams of life to the Miao churches

—an answer to eighteen months of prayer for revival by the women of the tribe.

The centre of the Miao work was at Kopu where there were 6,000 to 7,000 believers. The Church was rightly proud of its own industrial school for the blind. It also possessed the New Testament and a hymn book in their own tongue. A permanent Bible School remained in session for five months each year, and the neighbouring Nosu church shared the facilities of the school. The Gospel brought a stream of intelligence and spiritual enlightenment to the Miao tribes.

The burden of the tribes' work in south-west China has rested mainly on the shoulders of the C.I.M., although other missions had a share. In 1940, forty C.I.M. missionaries were at work in six different tribes.

In 1942 the Japanese Army overran Burma and advanced over the Chinese border as far as the Salween River. The Lisu missionaries had some narrow escapes from death and capture. Hollow Tree Church was occupied and the missionaries at Stockade Hill were temporarily cut off. The Burma Road, China's last lifeline, was severed, and a general panic sent refugees streaming up the Burma Road towards Kunming. The work at Oak Flat continued uninterrupted and as the danger receded the situation returned to normal. The Rainy Season Bible School for the Lisu was held as usual and students for the first Bible School for girls only came armed with note-books and pencils, prepared to take exams at the end. Certificates were proudly received on graduation day. The school ended, they returned to their mountain hamlets to teach others what they had learned. In 1941 the experiment of a United Tribes Bible School, first attempted unsuccessfully in 1937, was repeated. Ten tribes or sections of a tribe were represented at the school in Taku. Two years later the attendance reached a peak of thirty-seven, the students duplicating their own notes and lecture outlines. That year the first twelve men and women graduated.

A printing press for the special use of the tribes arrived in Kunming from the United States in 1947. Tribal workers had been seriously handicapped by the lack of suitable literature in their work. The new multi-lith duplicator was adaptable for a number of scripts. It was soon in service producing a catechism, a chorus book for the Lisu, a reader and hymn book in Tai and in Miao. Lisu New Testaments arriving from India and Shanghai were hailed with joy and speedily sold out.

A lone effort was made in 1940 to reach the Tuli tribe of Yunnan, related to the Lisu. But it came to nothing. Ten years later a further series of trips were made to these people living in the high ranges of west Yunnan. A few expressed faith in Christ but they had to be left prematurely with no one to teach them.

Early in 1949, in spite of difficult inland communications and the threatened Communist takeover, nine of the '48 group of recruits got away to west China. Two of them, Ernie and Mertie Heimbach, succeeded in reaching the old mission centre among the Black Miao at Panghsieh, the place where the first C.I.M. martyr died in 1899. Although it had been twelve years since any missionaries had been able to go to these people, the Heimbachs found a flickering light of testimony and a nucleus of faithful believers. Sadly, the missionaries came only to be withdrawn in 1951. The Black Miao were again without teachers.

The Communist Government was in effective control of most of China by 1950. In the Upper Salween the year began with fighting, uncertainty and doubt. But the February Bible School had a record attendance of ninety-eight students. Church growth was proceeding spontaneously and indigenously. In a changing society the Gospel and the Church were the only stable factors. Thirty Lisu teachers attended a Bible Study session in August—two refreshing weeks of fellowship at which Charles Peterson and John Kuhn assisted. The Lisu leaders themselves conducted over ten short-term Bible Schools during the year when many children came under instruction. November is the traditional month for harvest festivals and baptism: that year 100 were baptised. But the sands were running out for the tribal missionaries. That Christmas was their last. The glorious unaccompanied singing of the "Hallelujah Chorus" by 800 of these musical people was a memorable finale to foreign missionary endeavour among the tribes in China.

Orville Carlson, a worker among the Lisu, had already been appointed to start work across the River Salween in Burmese territory among the Lisu and the Maru Kachin tribes there. In 1950 he and his wife proceeded via Hong Kong and Rangoon and thence to Myitkyina by air. They immediately began to meet Lisu, some of whom were known to them. Goo-moo, the original Lisu village in Burma, was deserted because of a famine. The Christians had moved elsewhere. Years before these demon-worshippers, hearing that there were teachers of the true God over in China, had sent three men, at the very risk of their lives, floundering across the freezing, snowbound pass into the Salween Valley. There at Stockade Hill they had heard the Gospel and believed. Forthwith they carried the message back into Burma to their own people. As a result a vigorous Christian community sprang up among the Lisu and the related Maru were also evangelised. Goo-moo became the spiritual centre of a small group of chapels. Mark, one of the first three seekers, and the leader, in ten years led many to Christ before his death from malaria. By 1950 Christians were to be found everywhere. During the brief weeks of their visit the Carlsons visted as many Lisu, Maru and Saga as possible, to teach them the way more perfectly. They made their base in a Saga village where the 13,000-foot peaks of "the Hump" or the lower Himalayas towered above them and a mountain torrent foamed 2,000 feet below. The Christians built a temporary house for them, and provided food and milk. Seven weeks of fellowship was enjoyed with these Lisu and Maru Christians before the Carlsons had to leave. They had been able to make a start on the translation of a Saga Gospel—but it was left an unfinished task.

Similarly the whole task of evangelising the aboriginal groups in China was doomed to remain unfinished. Only a handful of the tribes had been effectively evangelised. And now the missionaries were about to leave China. Who would carry on the task? In Shanghai a large gathering of committed Christian students was presented with the challenge of their own countrymen—150 tribes waiting for the Gospel. The tribal surveys of Yunnan and Kweichow were translated into Chinese and distributed. A few Chinese Christians did respond and took up work in Yunnan among the tribes people. Their difficulties and problems were many and no recent news of their progress has been received.

The tribes churches themselves are known to have suffered greatly at the hands of the Communists. Many leaders were thrown into prison. Some died there. Others escaped over the high passes into Burma and settled down in new communities. As the work in north Thailand developed, Lisu Christians crossed over from Burma from time to time to help their foreign missionary friends. So did Akha Christians. Lahu Christians also moved over the border to escape the troubles in Burma. The Lisu church in Burma became strong. John Kuhn was able to visit them once or twice to minister to them. In north Thailand Alan Crane put the finishing touches to the complete translation of the Lisu Bible. In 1963 he, too, obtained permission to enter Burma to undertake the revision of the entire Old Testament with the help of the Lisu leaders. The Lisu church was eagerly looking forward to receiving their complete Bible some time in 1965. They began in 1963 to plan a Bible School especially to study the whole Bible, which would be in their hands for the first time. A well-established Church possessing both Old and New Testaments in one tribe only after fifty years! What of the remaining 149 tribes scattered like sheep over the mountains?

## CHAPTER 18

# THE UNCONQUERABLE

TIBET, land of mystery, has always been the inaccessible kingdom of devil-worshipping, buttered-tea-drinking lamas. Lhasa is the capital and the Potala is the ancient palace of the Dalai Lama. But few have ever reached the capital and fewer still have crossed the threshold of the palace. Range after range of lofty mountains are the natural ramparts of the kingdom. High snowbound passes where the step becomes slower and the lungs gasp for breath repel the most intrepid of travellers. On the border lands the nomads live in tents guarded by ferocious Tibetan hounds ready to tear to pieces any unauthorised intruder. Farther into the country there are ancient feudal castles and swashbuckling chieftains. Freebooting bandits also await the unwary traveller. Horses are the stock in trade and Tibetans are horsemen born: their reckless riding is a thrill to watch. These men are nourished on *tsampa*, the coarse barley which is all that the bleak and stony valleys can produce. *Tsampa*, the milk of the yak and the meat of the sheep are the diet of the Tibetan. His religion is Tantric Buddhism—more animistic than Buddhist. One son in each family is devoted to the priesthood and thus the whole land lies firmly in the grip of this comfortless religion.

.    .    .

*Flashback.* Ever since Dr. Cameron made his cautious way over the China border into Tibet in 1877 he has not lacked C.I.M. missionaries to follow in his trail. In 1897 Polhill Turner made Tatsienlu (Kangting) his base and the wild Tibetan border town remained a C.I.M.

centre until all missionaries left China. It had a population of Chinese, Tibetans and half-breeds. Like many a border town it had an evil reputation for gross immorality, official corruption and opium addiction. For the missionaries it was a suitable base for taking the Gospel to the Tibetans. The indomitable trio, Huston Edgar, Robert Cunningham and Theo Sorensen, the Norwegian scholar and translator, were unrivalled as travellers and evangelists and their knowledge of Tibet. The three men made frequent journeys into Tibet—to Litang, Batan, Deige-vouchen, Kanze and Daw until stringent regulations restricted free travel. Edgar travelled on the average 2,000 miles a year: he was constantly away from home, crossing 16,000-foot passes blocked with snow, trudging along great windswept valleys and sometimes bivouacking at night on the bleak mountainsides or risking the fierce mastiffs which guarded every home. But as the result of these journeys, the Tibetans became more friendly and the sales of Tibetan Scripture portions increased yearly. In 1924 Edgar actually sold 101,500 copies of the Scriptures and distributed 102,000 tracts in Tibetan. He was away from home for 181 days and 1,000 miles of his journeys were at 14,000–16,000 feet above sea-level.

In 1922 Sorensen set off on a journey to Lhasa. Like Annie Taylor he was turned back before reaching his goal. But on that trip alone he sold or distributed 60,000 Scripture portions.

About this time Dogget Learner opened an inn in Sining, the capital of the border province of Tsinghai, for the entertainment of Tibetans. One of the first converts, a half-Tibetan, was put in charge of the inn. Through his fearless witness to his fellow-countrymen, others were baptised. In near-by Lanchow, the leprosy wing of the Borden Memorial Hospital constantly received Tibetan sufferers, a number of whom trusted Christ and became firm believers.

Among those who responded to the appeal for the Two Hundred in 1929 were several who volunteered for work in Tibet. Ed Beatty and Dr. Howard Jeffery were appointed in 1938 to reach the Kiarung Tibetans, while

Virgil Hook went to the nomads of Tsinghai. The Kiarung language was then unknown to any foreigner. The road from the base at Mowkung into the Kiarung territory with its princes and castles crosses a pass as high as Mont Blanc. The Beattys joined the Jefferys in Mowkung for two months in 1940. But the ancient power of lamaism which had been one of Satan's fortresses for so long would yield only to a long siege. Medical work, the distribution of the Scriptures, the leprosarium in Lanchow and the Tibetan Gospel inn in Sining were all having a share in the preparation of Tibetan hearts for the Gospel. But results were disappointingly meagre. In 1942 Cunningham died after spending thirty-five years on the border.

The upheaval of the Sino-Japanese war gave new promise of a harvest among Tibetans. The Central Government began to take a greater interest in them and compulsory schools were established for Tibetan children. The lamas were conscripted to do national service. The Government insisted on government by the people and for the people instead of by the lamas for the lamas, changes which led to a greater friendliness towards the missionaries and a greater readiness to receive the Scriptures. The doors into Tibet were rudely jolted. Oddly enough the instruments of this jolting were sometimes the north-west Muslim officials, who on occasions sought to convert whole Tibetan communities to Islam.

The C.I.M. was working from three Tibetan centres in 1943: Kangting, Mowkung and Sining—but there was still no living church among the Tibetan people. Fifty miles west of Sining, Virgil Hook was enduring great hardships among the 40,000 Tibetan nomads; intense cold at over 13,000 feet above sea-level, life in a tent amid raging snowstorms, the constant discomforts of bugs, fleas and lice and the doubtful delicacies of buttered tea and ancient cuts of meat. The monastery town of Labrang was sometimes the starting place of these arduous journeys on which he had to carry his own tent and supplies—a task only for men prepared to endure real hardness. Contacts were made at Kumbum both with the boy Dalai Lama who accepted the Scriptures to read, and with the Panchen Lama, the second highest official in Tibet, who also accepted the Scriptures presented to him. Both men are now men of destiny, one a refugee in India, the other a tool of the Communists in Lhasa. Yet for the most part the Gospel has scarcely penetrated the Tibetan mind: Tibetans are still astonished at the idea that there is no value in the worship of Buddha.

In Kangting, where the altitude is 8,500 feet, missionaries have always taught the children either in a day school or a Sunday School. Many grown Tibetans have spoken appreciatively of the help so received in early years. In 1946 three C.I.M. couples joined Mrs. Cunningham. Geoffrey Bull and George Patterson of the Brethren also sojourned in the city for a time. Three sincere Chinese Christians completed the Christian community. Very good Sunday Schools and children's services were held during the week, most of the children in the day school being Tibetans. But it was not only children who came under the sound of the Gospel. The holocaust of war brought many Tibetans out from their mountain fastnesses to hear the Gospel. Was the price of faith too great? Was the memory too vivid of the Christian convert who was sewn into a fresh yak skin by merciless priests and placed in the broiling sun until the contraction of the skin squeezed the life out of his frame? In Kangting slides on the life of Christ provided a great attraction and sometimes as many as 100 at a time stood to listen and watch: men with long swords, picturesque garb and typical Tibetan swagger listening intently to the story of the Man who will one day be King of the World. A census showed that almost every province of Tibet was represented; some having travelled for months to reach Kangting. Access to people from all parts of Tibet was in this way gained. Even Lhasa-trained monks, conscious of their special prestige, talked earnestly about the Lord Jesus Christ. But believe? Never! Was faith then impossible for Tibetans? No, for all things are possible with God: in 1948 an old Chinese lady and a Tibetan girl boldly confessed Christ in baptism.

Meanwhile at Hwalung on the Kansu-Tibetan frontier, the Holy Light School organisation sponsored a twelve-bed hospital, an outreach of the Lanchow Hospital. The clinic gained rapid fame, especially when a Living Buddha with his entire encampment arrived with fifty men requiring treatment and forty needing operations. At the hospital even more Tibetans came under medical care and the sound of the Gospel.

But the Communist armies were heading for north-west China and in August 1949 Lanchow fell. The hospital and the Hwalung clinic were permitted to continue for a time, then both were taken over, and the missionaries left for the coast. Dr. Rupert Clarke, accused of manslaughter for failing to save the life of a dying man, lingered on under solitary house arrest. Nevertheless, the witness had not been in vain. It was the joy of George Bell and Norman McIntosh, Tibetan workers, before leaving Kansu to baptise two south Tibetan women who gave true signs of faith in God— the first Tibetan baptisms in the north-west for twenty-eight years.

Nor was that the end of the story. In the same year that Dr. Rupert Clarke was released the witness of a group of Chinese Christians in Labrang resulted in twenty professions of faith. The event was so news-worthy that it was reported by Tibetans in India. And the story continues. The revised Tibetan Bible became a standard work of correct modern Tibetan. The first edition of 1,000 copies was widely distributed and freely read. When Communist soldiers needed a text-book from which to study the Tibetan language, the Tibetan Bible was used. People are also hearing the Gospel from gramophone records purchased in India. Many a Tibetan travelling over rocky passes or huddled sheltering from the blizzards has heard on his transistor receiving-set Gospel programmes from Taiwan or Okinawa, which prompts them to ask as they come down into India, "Who is this Jesus Christ they talk about?"

The early missionaries to Tibet dared to believe that the conversion of Tibetans was possible. There are now

Christians and possibly even one local church in Tibet. The unconquerable kingdom has already been politically conquered. Highways are carrying men and merchandise from China into the heart of Tibet. Could these also become highways of the Gospel as Chinese Christians, too, travel over the highways—a highway for our God? The impossible is happening.

## CHAPTER 19

# A CLUSTER OF IMPOSSIBLES

THE C.I.M., immediately after V.J. Day, sent for twenty men from the home countries to form "comfort" teams to visit the churches which had been under Japanese occupation. Letters were sent ahead to convey the Mission's affectionate greetings. The teams followed with a commission to exercise a ministry of comfort to those who had passed through great trials and to find out what the churches now required of the Mission—if anything. Teams went to Chekiang, Kiangsi, Anhwei, Honan and to the still accessible areas of Hopeh and Shansi, where parts were already under Communist control. The reception given to the missionaries after several years of separation was without exception heart-warming. Even non-Christians were enthusiastic in their welcome and invitations were often given to speak in schools and prisons. On the whole the teams were encouraged with what they found. Despite some sad losses, the churches had held their ground. Scarcely any had closed down. Many were strongly steadfast, while in some areas a remarkable work of God had taken place.

In Honan 1,800 baptisms had taken place during the two years' absence of the missionaries. In the Swedish Mission field along the Yellow River Valley, a revived Church had attracted 2,000 additional new members and the membership of one church alone grew from 300 to 1,000 during 1946. The teams held important conferences with the church leaders; even in Shansi, where conditions were most difficult, 145 delegates were able to meet in Hungtung, and they too reported 1,000 baptisms during the war years. In Fowyang, Anhwei, heart of a great agricultural area, a small mass-movement had been started: five pastors had been appointed to supervise the fifty central and seventy-five country churches. Congregations of over 1,000 crowded into the city church on Sundays and services were being held nightly through the week. In Shaohsing, Chekiang, called the "Ephesus" of China because of its idol industry, and noted for its opposition to the Gospel, the church leaders were rejoicing in 200 recent conversions and the doubling of the church's membership. In Szechwan the Anglican diocese after fifteen years of great progress celebrated its Jubilee in 1945; a Chinese synod then assumed full responsibility for the diocese. In Kiangsi, after years of terrible suffering under both the Communists and the Japanese, the Church was very much alive.

To the question "Are the missionaries welcome to return?" (which was not taken for granted), the answer was unequivocal:

"Of course we want you to come back. We desperately need your help. The number of Chinese with your training and experience is far too few and will continue to be so for a long time to come. But we must respectfully make this clear. For four or five years we have been managing on our own and under tremendous difficulties. God has taught us many valuable lessons of trust in Him. Now there can be no going back to the pre-war situation when we were dependent on you. You missionaries must not think of coming back to control us. We have developed under the Japanese occupation into really autonomous churches and we desire to remain so. But there are so many ways in which we need your assistance: in Bible teaching, Sunday School work, leadership training and in other specialised ministries. If you are prepared to come and work in fellowship with us and even under our authority, you will be more than welcome." This at least was the gist of what was said in many places. So the pattern for Missions as they faced the uncertain future in 1946 became plain: the task of evangelism and church building was no longer one that solely concerned the missionary, but one in which the whole church must share.

As requests for the help of missionaries began to pour in it became clear that all could not possibly be met. Less than half the Mission's personnel had returned to China, including the fifty-three recruits who sailed in 1946 and who would not be effective immediately. Some of these, trained in London amid air-raids and rocket attacks, had been waiting since 1943. In view of the great need, the Directors' Conference in Shanghai in 1947 recognised the necessity to double the number of missionaries if all the calls were to be met. The Directors therefore issued an appeal for "recruits of the highest calibre, men of spiritual freshness and power, ready to function immediately in any circumstances, men who are attracted by the Cross and nothing else, and who have already learned something of what it means to die to self in all its forms; men of initiative and ideas yet so disciplined that the Chinese whom they have inspired will imagine that the ideas are their own—men and women of tried spiritual quality and of the humility which rejoices to lead by serving".

.    .    .

In spite of the threat of Communist victory the Mission did not lack experienced men who were still fired with a passion for the humanly impossible. There remained in China one oustanding challenge to the pioneer missionary, the very impossibility of which was irresistible. Walled-in behind the wide moat of the River of Golden Sands, as the Yangtze is called in its upper reaches, and stretching west to the border of Tibet, is the forbidding land of the "Independent" Nosu (or Lolo), a mountain territory of wild tribesmen which strangers enter at their peril. They are a feudal people with hereditary ranks and territories, with princes, nobles, gentlemen and ladies, as dignified as they are indolent, having their teeming serfs and freemen tenants. Their carved and ornamented medieval halls, hung with skins and weapons, are barbaric in appearance as the lurid flames from the log fires light up the warriors clad in red buckskin and bristling with arms. It is all very picturesque if one forgets the sordid background of dirt and bloodlust. Opium smoking and wine drinking are both widespread and an equal curse. There have always been severe travel restrictions imposed by Chinese and Nosu alike to prevent free entry. Indeed, travel was only possible if accompanied by a friendly chief as a sort of living passport to guarantee safety. "Life," wrote someone about these people, "is a rough and tumble and a bloody jest."

These people had never been effectually reached by the Word of Life in the many centuries of their existence. In 1903 Sam Pollard paid a ten-day visit from the Methodist field in the east. Brief visits were paid about the same time by Cook and King of the C.I.M. King lived for some years on the northern border of Lolo territory. Chinese scientific and social service teams have paid visits, but no more than a handful of foreigners had ever crossed the borders and one of these, Lieutenant Francis Brook, an explorer, was murdered in 1908. Was it remotely possible that anything could be done so late in the day? Dr. Jim Broomhall thought "yes". He was, after all, the grandson of the founder's sister and had the blood of pioneers in his veins.

So Broomhall, with a Chinese companion, reached Sichang, the western gateway of Nosuland, a sizeable and important city, in April 1947. There three weeks of detailed and careful preparations were necessary before they scaled the mountains of the Promised Land. Then for forty-five days they travelled within Nosu borders, more than three times as long a visit as any previous foreign visitor had paid. Everywhere they met with a warm reception and at Chaokioh, the walled town in the very centre of the Taliangshan, the great mountain range of Nosuland, Broomhall's plan to come and live among them and to start a small hospital was enthusiastically hailed with acclamation. To set His seal on the project, God called and moved the heart of the interpreter, a Nosu of the upper class, to believe unto salvation three weeks after hearing the Gospel for the first time. Broomhall now set about completing his team for the task: the missionaries were Janet his wife, Ruth

Dix and Joan Wales, and for a few months only, Floyd Larsen, well experienced on the Tibetan border. A few Chinese and Nosu Christians completed the team. Sichang was established as a supply base. In April 1948, the party reached Chaokioh, the chosen centre, four days from Sichang by mule. A delegation of officials extended a ceremonial welcome. Buildings for a residence and a clinic were acquired inside the walls of the ancient fort. Early in 1949 the ladies joined the men, while building operations and medical work began simultaneously. In April the three Broomhall children were taken into Chaokioh against all the pleadings of people of experience in Sichang. But for the Broomhalls, this enterprise was the beginning of their life work, and Chaokioh was to be their home. It was natural for the children to be there too. At Easter 1949 the church in Chaokioh—consisting of the five missionaries only—celebrated the death and Resurrection of Christ. On Easter Day fifty persons actually joined them for the Easter service and thus regular services began.

Are there any rivers you think are uncrossable?
Are there any mountains you cannot tunnel through?
God specialises in the wholly impossible,
Doing the things which man cannot do.

But the creeping Communist occupation of China could not be concealed from the people of Nosuland nor ignored by the missionaries. Inevitably, even Chaokioh was occupied by Communist troops in April 1949. But the preaching of Christ in the villages and the ministering to the sick went on. In June two nineteen-year-old girls and an older woman believed. One or two others, locals and Chinese, joined the little company of Christians until there were twelve genuine inquirers after the Truth, eager to be taught the Way more perfectly. All around them was unspeakable wickedness. Violence often erupted. But unflaggingly they studied the faith and grew in the knowledge of Christ. The Communist soldiers denounced the missionaries as imperialist spies, but a Communist indoctrinator who challenged Broomhall as a deceiver became a seeker himself and accepted a New Testament. A leader of the "tame" Nosu church at Salowu paid one visit to Nosuland, and hopes were high that he might return to conduct a baptismal service at Christmas time. But he failed to get through. The baptisms never took place. Christmas was celebrated as joyfully as possible and the story of the birth of Christ told again. But on that very Christmas night there were rumours that the foreigners would be killed and their children taken as slaves. Despite the persistent rumours, the medical workers went on caring for the sick, including Communist soldiers, until the feared and fateful order to withdraw came from Shanghai. As the missionaries prepared to leave the local people showed great sorrow and the demonstrations of affection were touching in the extreme. In the past nine months as many as thirty men, women, girls and boys had made profession of faith in Christ. In January 1950 the sad little cavalcade left a weeping Christian group behind as they began the long journey for Sichang, Chengtu and the coast.

. . .

In 1945 it would have seemed beyond the realm of possibility that Chinese university students would be crowding the theological colleges and offering themselves as poor and despised missionaries to their own peoples along China's western border. It was not long since they had been the most bitterly anti-Christian elements in the country. But the impossible happened. And the most thrilling work in China in the short postwar years was that among the students and the young people of the country. Missionaries had realised that the true test of events which transpired while students were refugees in the west would come when they returned to their own campuses in the great eastern cities of China and met again the temptations of materialism, the challenge of Communism and the emasculated Gospel of theological liberalism. There were naturally some misgivings. But the China Inter-Varsity Fellowship quickly set up an office in Nanking under David Adeney's direction. Invitations from students in Shanghai, Hankow, Wuchang, Changsha, Chengtu, Chungking, Sian and Peking to supply missionary student workers were met as far as possible by some of the Mission's more experienced student workers. In Peking alone there were six universities and three colleges of university status besides technical colleges of various kinds with a total of 15,000 students. Disappointed with a powerless formalism and having had a taste of vital Christianity, students everywhere literally pressed into the Kingdom. There were baptisms in large numbers. Fellowship meetings lasted for hours as scores of young men and women shared with others the joys and testings of their new-found faith. The local organisations were entirely in the hands of the students themselves. Bible classes, gatherings for prayer, fellowship meetings and evangelism all found a place in the weekly programme. Students were urged to establish a close link with a local church. Some meetings were held on the university campus, while joint activities were held in a neutral building. In the summer and winter the students arranged special conferences—under the shadow of the walls of the Summer Palace outside Peking, on the hills above Chungking or in the flat and unlovely suburbs of Shanghai. An air of revival characterised all these gatherings. Deep conviction of sin was common. Real and lasting conversions were many. Christians evidenced a joy and an enthusiasm which surprised university circles all over China. Who can forget the sight of truck-loads of Christian students riding through the streets of Peking singing Christian songs with the same fervour which had once characterised their anti-Christian demonstrations in this very ancient capital, the city whose students traditionally set the pattern for all universities? Many a student revolutionary movement had started there. Was this yet another?

The new movement rather naturally was bitterly attacked by agencies like the left-wing Y.M.C.A. which had previously enjoyed a monopoly of student work. They found it hard to understand how the C.I.V.F. movement could survive without highly-paid secretaries, student centres and the generous distribution of relief funds which were the backbone of their own work. But lacking any of these the C.I.V.F. invaded university after university, where students were converted and new fellowships formed. In 1947 the greatest conference of evangelical students ever to be held in China met on "Purple Mountain" outside Nanking. There were 200 delegates from 100 universities and colleges. The First Lady of the Land paid a visit and expressed her own Christian sympathy with the new movement. The demand for periodicals and books suited to the student mind, both in English and in Chinese, was insistent. The recent translation of *Hudson Taylor* by a Chinese doctor provided a very popular best-seller, and another book by a Chinese C.I.V.F. secretary on the philosophy of Communism and Christianity called *Questions of Faith* had an even wider circulation. On graduation some students were going to the border regions as missionaries to their own people. Evangelical church leaders firmly supported the movement which contained the promise of great things for the Church in China. All of them spent much time with the students. The tragic mass exodus of students from areas occupied by the Communists, especially from Manchuria, brought thousands to Peking where in freezing temperatures they were billeted in draughty temples or in the open courtyards of the Temple of Heaven and the Confucian temple. There the local Christian students held evangelistic meetings for them and ministered in practical ways to their physical needs. Many conversions resulted. Even as the Communist armies closed in on Peking, and city after city fell, there was no lessening of the tempo. Other Christian student organisations saw in the Communist programme the realisation of their own ideals and threw in their lot with the Communists, but these students were prepared for arrest, imprisonment and trial as they continued to witness courageously and uncompromisingly for Christ.

Two such Christians in a Chungking prison one day began to sing "Rock of Ages" in their crowded cell. The other prisoners then invited them to speak about their Christian faith. The New Testament which they had managed to keep was passed round and read: conversions resulted. A Christian guard smuggled in a complete Bible for the student who had given up his own New Testament. During the sixty-three days of his captivity he read it right through. On New Year's Day all the prisoners in the jail joined in a Christian service.

Such was the impetus of this movement that the Communists did not arrest it until 1955, although the C.I.V.F. organisation officially disbanded in 1951. It is doubtful if the movement has been halted even now, for all over China there are those who can never forget those wonderful years before "liberation" when their lives were revolutionised by the power of Christ. They constitute oases amid the arid deserts of materialism.

## CHAPTER 20

# NO GOD BUT ALLAH

ISLAM reached China in the eighth century. Its chief strongholds are in the north-west and the south-west, although there are Muslim communities in every large city of China—about 10 million Muslims in all. Chinese Muslims have a distinct culture of their own. They are a people apart with a strong community spirit and the binding ties of a common social system. When the Christian missionary seeks to invade their ancient stronghold with the Christian message, he faces another well-nigh impossible task. It is "impenetrable as walls of brass". Temple Gardiner of Cairo in his book *The Rebuke of Islam* writes: "Islam is the impossible-possible problem". And C.I.M. missionaries among Muslims have always shown a passion for and a patience in attempting the impossible. In the north-west, where Islam has gained political power, the proud figure of a Muslim on his spirited Arab steed was a typical symbol of Islam's unique place in Chinese life.

.    .    .

*Flashback* The first C.I.M. missionary to discover the Muslims of the north-west was Dr. Cameron as he visited Kansu and Central Asia. The Muslims in Kansu, Tsinghai and Ninghsia early became the concern of the C.I.M. There were so many of them that it was impossible even for Chinese workers to ignore them. Then specialists began to preach the Gospel to the *imâms* in the mosques and to Muslims everywhere. The Botham family devoted their lives to evangelism of the Muslims. Death cut short the life and service of Mark Botham. Nineteen children's graves could once be seen in the Lanchow cemetery—the graves of children of missionaries to the Muslims. But Muslim converts numbered less than this!

William Borden, the young millionaire and Yale university student, heard the call of the Muslims of north-west China and responded. He reached Egypt on his way with the intention of studying Islam at first hand before going to China. But there his life ended. The hospital in Lanchow was built in his memory, and with his money. It became in a special sense a witness to the Muslims. Through the corn of wheat that died more Muslims have found Christ there than anywhere else in the north-west. It was, for the most part, as lepers coming to the leprosarium that they and Tibetans found in Christ a common Saviour.

The call of the "great north-west" was strong. In 1914 Percy Mather went to join Hunter in Sinkiang and at once became an equally dauntless apostle of the steppes. In 1923 Mildred Cable, Eva and Francesca French heard the call and the "Trio", with twenty to thirty years' work in Shansi behind them, ventured to the even needier "pan-handle" area of Kansu. They chose to live at Suchow, the last city before Jade Gate, the border post between Turkestan and Kansu. It was there that the great caravans assembled down through history before continuing their journey along the Old Silk Road across the Gobi Desert to Central Asia and India. Six weeks' journey away to the north-west lived Hunter and Mather at Urumchi. For fifteen years the Trio travelled constantly around their vast and lonely parish "gossiping the Gospel" wherever they went. During those hazardous years of Muslim revolts and civil war, they undertook five epic journeys through and in the "New Province". *Through Jade Gate* (1927) and *Desert Journal* (1934) are classics of travel literature. When they returned to England to retire the Queen received them at Buckingham Palace. They were also awarded the Lawrence of Arabia Medal of the Royal Central Asian Society and the Livingstone Medal of the Royal Scottish Geographical Society.

In 1926 Ridley joined Hunter and Mather, later to be

followed by the six of the Two Hundred. After the sad losses of Mather and Fischbacher, Harold Hayward, a new arrival in 1935, wrote from Urumchi: "No field seems so barren of results as the Muslim world." For many years the membership of the church at Urumchi remained at about six. The arrest of Hunter by the Russians in 1939 was a severe setback to the little group. He was held prisoner for eighteen months and suffered torture at the hands of the N.K.V.D. to extract a confession of being a spy. One day, in 1941, the Eurasian Air Corporation in Lanchow sent word to the Mission that an old man was due to arrive from Hami by plane. What a welcome George Hunter received, and how he pored over a Bible after being denied one for over a year! But after a few weeks in comparative comfort recovering from the effects of his imprisonment, the indomitable veteran set off once more for Kanchow, near the Sinkiang border. There, at eighty-five years of age, he died in 1946, lonely in death as he had been in life. Yet he had not lived in vain. Others reaped where he had sowed. In 1941 one stream of the great migration of intelligentsia from Japanese-occupied territory flowed into Central Asia. Christians were among them. The church in Tihwa grew out of all recognition. Muslims for the first time began to hear the Gospel from intelligent Chinese Christians and some were converted. The coming of educated people from the East introduced new influences, disturbing and disruptive as far as Islam was concerned.

Back in Sining, George Harris had set himself to master the Arabic language and to become an expert in the Koran. Neither the meat nor the fat of the pig forbidden to a Muslim ever crossed his threshold and, knowing this, Muslims did not hesitate to pay him many a visit. His scholarship gained increasing respect; many *ahungs* and *mullahs* heard the Gospel from Harris and his fellow-workers. In 1936 Dr. Samuel Zwemer, the Muslim expert, visited the north-west and brought great encouragement to them all. There he met Ma—an *ahung* and one of the best-educated Muslims in Kansu, whom he found to be a soul in misery because of his sin. While a patient in the Borden Memorial Hospital he had begun to study the Bible. The day came when he signified his willingness to confess his Christian faith publicly by baptism in the Yellow River in the presence of hundreds of Muslim onlookers. His relatives immediately attempted to kill him by poisoning, but only succeeded in temporarily affecting his mind. As soon as he recovered he began to visit Muslim tea shops in the city where, like the Apostle Paul, he boldly preached the faith he had once opposed. "What is your answer to the stock Muslim objections?" someone asked him. Holding up his Bible, he replied "This book!" In 1944 Harris produced a *Manual for workers among Muslims* as a further contribution to their evangelisation. The Yunnan Muslims shared the ignorance and misunderstanding of their brethren in the north-west. They were courteous, but they were suspicious and afraid of any kind of Christian activity.

When the war ended, the church situation in the north-west and Central Asia was very different. Thriving churches were found in all the main towns of Sinkiang—living churches which Muslims could observe for the first time since the days of the Nestorians. The postmaster of Urumchi and his wife were active Christians. So were two high Government officials—both generals. The Urumchi church consisting of forty baptised members was therefore invited to meet in the hall of the Party headquarters. Christians could also be found working in the oil-fields on the Kansu border. The Muslims could not fail to be aware of them. The Central Evangelistic Team of Kansu included Ma—the converted *ahung* and so a former Muslim scholar was actively preaching Christ to Muslims. Muslims were thinking deeply: one young man said to a missionary, "Our religion might not be the true one!"—a straw in the wind, but the opportunities were great. George Harris was invited to visit a Muslim college, a veritable citadel of Islam. There he gave an address and afterwards gave out Bibles, New Testaments and Gospel portions; when his supply was exhausted, there were requests for more! Incidentally in 1951 Muslim leaders in Shanghai actually visited the C.I.M. headquarters to ask for Christian apologetic literature to help them in their defence against atheistic materialism!

Then a remarkable thing happened. A former ardent Nationalist by the common name of Ma, with the Christian name of Mark, was vice-principal of the North-West Bible Institute in Shensi, of which Hudson Taylor's grandson was the Principal. There God gave him the vision of preaching the Gospel right through the Muslim lands of Central Asia and carrying it back to Jerusalem from where it originated. The "Back to Jerusalem Band" was formally inaugurated in 1946, with 600 Christians undertaking the support of eight full-time Chinese missionaries in this work. Mark Ma set about studying Arabic under George Harris in preparation for his task! The time was ripe: many hearts were sick and hungry and weary of mere religion. They wanted a living Saviour. In 1954 news reached the outside world of two further Muslim converts going as missionaries to their own people in Central Asia, while at Tihwa a converted Muslim was teaching fourteen students in a Bible School. On Easter Day 1954, five years after the Communist takeover of China, the Church in Tihwa baptised nineteen people.

Far away in Hong Kong, in a refugee camp, missionaries discovered a fine, educated man who had once been prominent in the leadership of his Muslim faith, but was now a true Christian. Over in Taiwan, Eric Liberty, a former Kansu missionary, met yet another Muslim trophy of grace who had been converted to Christ in the north-west of China. He was still a faithful and consistent Christian. Indeed the work has not been in vain, and Islam is still stretching out its hands to the living God.

## CHAPTER 21

# ANOTHER TWILIGHT

ONE of the foremost Chinese leaders of the Church—the
Rev. Marcus Cheng—was convinced that during the
war God's Church in China reached the time of harvest.
But he saw also that her greatest need was for trained
leaders. West China had next to no local leadership. If
the proportion of Christians in east China was 1 in 360,
in west China it was only 1 in 3,500. The supreme need
was for Chinese evangelists to reach the masses, of which
Szechwan province alone contained 45 million. In 1944
Marcus Cheng accepted the Principalship of the Chungking Theological Seminary with the strong moral
support of the C.I.M. Its financial policy was one of faith
in God so as to better train the students in the life of
simple trust in the living God. By 1947 there were
seventy-nine students, of whom fifty were men. The
students represented fifteen provinces and included three
tribal Christians. Some of these men were converts from
Communism. Eight C.I.M. missionaries were on the
staff. The visit of the Home Directors to the Seminary in
1947 was marked by a spiritual awakening. The students
took part in no more fruitful work in Chungking than
that which had begun in the city prison. A surprising
response to the Gospel came from among the murderers,
traitors, opium addicts, bandits, counterfeiters and
whoremongers found there. Lives were revolutionised,
and altogether over 200 were baptised. A church in the
prison came into existence, and the work spread to
another prison through the witness of prisoners. But this
unusual development gained too much publicity in the
Press; the Christian jailer was dismissed, and replaced
by an ardent Buddhist.

Other new colleges were started in several provinces, and the C.I.M. gladly supplied staff members. In Anhwei, the Wuhu Bible Institute made a promising start; then, when the school was threatened with closure, it began a correspondence course in which 950 students from thirteen provinces rapidly enrolled. In Lanchow, the Spiritual Training Institute had forty students in 1950.

In Shanghai C.I.M. missionaries were teaching in the China Bible Seminary, whose 500 graduates were scattered throughout all China and South-east Asia. Two of the more recent were members of the team on the edge of Nosuland. Latterly there were ninety students, half of them men, and many of them university graduates. It was almost a new thing for university graduates, able to command a large salary and a good position in the country, to sacrifice those prospects for the service of Christ and His Church. The supply of teaching staff by the Mission to seventeen colleges was a strategic ministry at a critical time.

.    .    .

Missionaries of an earlier generation would scarcely have believed that mass evangelism on a large scale could ever come to China. But it did. All knew that it was a race against time for the soul of a nation. The methods of the Pocket Testament League and of Youth for Christ inspired the church and missionaries to herculean efforts. Trucks equipped with loud-speakers made it possible to bring whole cities under the sound of the Gospel and this was frequently done. With the co-operation of the military authorities a very widespread distribution of John's Gospel was carried out by the Pocket Testament League in which C.I.M. missionaries took part: 35,000 soldiers in Shanghai, 20,000 in Nan-king, 2,000 in Hangchow not only received the Gospels but were paraded to listen to a simple presentation of the Christian message. This was repeated from city to city with the goodwill of the military authorities.

C.I.M. missionaries were also loaned to Youth for

Christ and participated in city-wide campaigns up and down the country. One of the most interesting was in Peking, where a huge mat auditorium was erected on the historic embassy polo ground near the Hatamen Gate. Thousands of people listened to the Gospel nightly for ten days—probably the largest evangelistic mission of its kind ever attempted in Peking, and certainly the last. There were many conversions as the result of systematic follow-up work. Not long after, that same polo ground became an emergency airfield in defence against the Communist armies. In Tienshui, Kansu, where 3,000 people listened to the Gospel, 300 made decisions for Christ. Three hundred also made decisions in Lanchow. In other north-western cities 10,000 to 20,000 people stood each Saturday night in the public square to hear the Gospel. In one place, 13,000 stood in the pouring rain for two hours so eager were they to hear. In the south-west the largest available theatres were packed out twice nightly to hear the Truth about Jesus Christ. University and High school students were prominent in the crowds. High schools were opened up to the evangelists and in one school alone 297 made decisions for Christ. The youth of China was open to the Gospel as never before and the churches were aware of the opportunity. No one had ever seen the like. In two centres in Kweichow an open-air campaign resulted in 220,000 people hearing the Gospel in the course of fifty-seven hours of preaching. In one meeting 5,000 stood in the rain for three hours listening intently. The tide was at the flood.

The burning question in the minds of the C.I.M. directors was whether at such a time of grave crisis there was justification for bringing further recruits to China. To human reason the idea was almost preposterous. Already the consular officials were saying to the '48 group, "What a time to come to China!" The Communist armies were gaining success after success. What purpose was there in bringing fresh reinforcements to China now? But faith obeys where it cannot see, and God had His secret purposes when the waiting party received directions to proceed to Hong Kong *en route* for

Chungking in west China. Houses on the Chungking hills were prepared for a language school. No time was wasted in Hong Kong and the party flew almost at once across war-torn China and touched down on the sandbank landing-strip in the river. Almost immediately the route closed behind them as the Hong Kong-Chungking air service was suspended—a miracle of divine timing. Only the future could justify the decision taken.

But the shadows were drawing in. Financial chaos and social insecurity were causing widespread student unrest and actual starvation among the very poor. The Central Government had completely lost the confidence of the nation. The army was demoralised. Peking fell in November 1948. Then in 1949, as the Nationalist régime cracked, Nanking fell in April, Shanghai in May, Lanchow in August, Canton in October, Kweiyang and Chungking in November. The newly-arrived recruits on the Chungking hills found themselves in the midst of the battle for the city. These campaigns involved a fearful toll of suffering, death and destruction throughout China. The Nationalist Government took refuge in Taiwan (Formosa), the island province recovered in 1945 from the Japanese. But on the mainland the People's Government was firmly established. If the revolution of 1926–7 had been an explosion, violent and evanescent, this revolution of 1948 was an avalanche, ponderous, irresistible and conclusive.

For the time being missionary work continued. At the end of 1949 there were still 737 members of the Mission in China. Local withdrawals were sometimes necessary, but they usually meant a change of station only. Yet there was little to relieve the gloom. In Shansi a Swedish associate lady missionary and a Chinese elder faced a Communist tribunal and were added to the roll of martyrs. Other missionaries suffered violent deaths at the hands of lawless men. Churches were closing. Lesser Communist officials sometimes confiscated Bibles and imprisoned pastors. In spite of the new situation, large numbers of people, especially students, were being baptised all over China. Increasing restrictions on travel confined most of the 1948 recruits to Shanghai without any hope of moving inland. Only nine of their year got away to the West. Missionary work in China was plainly in its final stages.

1950 was a year of pressure on foreign missionaries. Chinese Christians evidenced a growing fear of man and of the future, as their hospitals, schools and orphanages were taken over by the Government. The Shanghai Christian broadcasting station was ordered to close down. The authorities used the war in Korea to inflame popular opinion against the West, especially after China became involved. The slow, relentless tide moved steadily in, pushing, squeezing, pressing against the Church and the missionary body. The C.I.M. faced extinction.

In May 1950 Mr. Chou En-lai invited a group of self-appointed Chinese Christian leaders to meet him in Peking. The meeting produced a Manifesto, dictated by Chou but purporting to express the feelings of the whole Church in China. In it the Church agreed to purge itself of all "imperialist" influences and to accept the leadership of the Communist Party. When this tragic meeting was reported to a representative gathering of missionaries and Christian leaders in Shanghai in May 1950, the writing on the wall as far as foreign missionaries were concerned was plain for all to read. On May 26th, "*Lammermuir* Day", John Sinton, the acting China Director, cabled all the Home centres: "Pray. Possibly facing the darkest period in Mission's history. But what saith the answer of God?" The Government clearly intended that all foreigners should go. But they were to be invited to leave by the churches and not ordered out by the Government. Pressure was therefore brought to bear on missionaries throughout the country to refrain from attending church worship, to cease their Bible classes and to avoid "embarrassing" their Chinese friends and colleagues. The continued presence of the missionary was now an acute embarrassment and a positive hindrance to the Christian community. One by one Missions made the reluctant decision to withdraw their staffs from China. Han Su-yin, the Chinese novelist, puts into the mouth of an ex-missionary the words, "Missionaries will never go back to China . . . it is no use deluding ourselves. We have done our work and now we must go. Some will be clinging on until one by one they too will drop off. The China Inland Mission will probably stay on a little longer. And the Catholic Church will hang on to the end." Her prophecy was true.

The second fateful telegram in which John Sinton informed the home countries that, as co-operation with the churches was no longer possible and Chinese Christians were suffering for their association with the missionaries, gradual withdrawal of all missionaries would begin, was dispatched on December 12th. Before the end of the year 185 members were advised to leave. As the anti-imperialist movement swept the country this modified withdrawal changed to a policy of total evacuation. The decision was epoch making. It implied the complete winding-up of the Mission in China. When the Chefoo School in Kuling was ordered to disband, the death knell of the Mission in China was sounded. As the year closed 518 full members, 119 associate members and a large number of children were still dispersed throughout the country. How would they fare as they requested permission to leave? How would the immense cost of the evacuation be met? And what did the future hold for them all?

One bright shaft of light which shone into the darkness of the Shanghai headquarters at this time was the visit of a group of Christians from Hopeh. They had been without missionary fellowship since 1939, but had survived the war with Japan and all its dangers and experienced the early Communist occupation. Now, hearing that the missionaries were about to leave, they came to see their old friends again and to say good-bye. They were tried and tested warriors. Having faced privations, imprisonment, persecution and death for Christ, their faith was stronger than ever. They had seen signs following the preaching of God's Word: demons exorcised and the dying restored to life before the eyes of sceptical materialists. One of them conducted an industrial Bible School—teaching a trade by day and the Bible by night to men and women who would later ply their trade and preach the Gospel at the same time. The day of professional preachers was drawing to an end. If the missionaries had to go, they took comfort in the knowledge that there were mature and courageous Christian men and women who would take up the torch of the faith and hand it on.

1951 became a story of retreat. The heavy cost of the great withdrawal was met in two ways: by wonderfully large incomes in 1950 and 1951, but even more miraculously by the successful renting of the valuable headquarters premises in Shanghai to a Communist Government hospital, together with the outright sale of the furniture. Humanly speaking the transaction was a sheer impossibility. The Government had demanded the deeds of every foreign property throughout China. It could easily have expropriated these premises in the same way, without compensation. The missionaries were on the way out and it was only a matter of time before the premises would fall naturally into their hands. But the God of the impossible again intervened and inclined the People's Government of China to sign a rental agreement with the C.I.M. to pay out the huge sum of £28,570. This was enough to cover the entire cost of the withdrawal to the coast of every missionary, the severance pay demanded by hundreds of Chinese employees whose livelihood was lost by the departure of the missionaries, and the support of the missionaries who were detained after the main body had left. The deal was made against the wishes of powerful men who were, however, helpless to stop it. The current income was therefore kept in Hong Kong to cover the cost of passages home and other current expenses. God is still a miracle-working God.

But 600 missionaries and their children had to be accommodated in an already grossly overcrowded Hong Kong. Shipping was scarce and long delays were inevitable. Hotels, schools, church guest-houses and boarding-houses were out of the question. But God again intervened. After every imaginable possibility had been investigated by people who knew Hong Kong well, someone heard about a semi-dismantled army camp of eleven Nissen huts within a stone's throw of the Mission's temporary headquarters in Chatham Road, but hidden in an obscure area down by the sea, which would exactly meet the need. The water and the electricity had already been cut off and the site was derelict. This situation was soon remedied and the whole place speedily transformed into a reception centre. Two hundred and fifty camp beds and 600 blankets seemed to arrive from nowhere, and a catering staff was installed. The camp was christened "Freehaven" and the Chefoo School children were among the first to take occupation. After that the stream of evacuees never ceased to flow. Hong Kong became a haven of relief and a place of rest where 600 missionaries, utterly weary after harrowing experiences at the hands of the Communists and many a hair-raising journey, relaxed and waited. "It is impossible to find any accomodation in Hong Kong!" they said. But it wasn't!

By April 1951, the number of missionaries in China was reduced to 371. At the end of June it was 203. In September it fell to ninety and by the end of the year it was thirty-three. Those who were left behind were haunted by loneliness and foreboding. They were cut off, harassed, maltreated, humiliated, reduced to penury, denied the necessities of life, confined and even imprisoned for longer or short periods of time. David Day was confined with twenty-one other men in a cell measuring twelve feet square. No talking was permitted and each man was allowed to stand up for fifteen minutes daily. Don Cunningham was imprisoned, while his wife and children were turned out of their home and forced to beg for food on the streets. Don spent nine months in prison before breathing fresh air again. Other stories have been told in full elsewhere.* But at long last all got safely out of China without any loss of life. Roman Catholic missionaries were far less fortunate. The last members of the C.I.M. and almost the last Protestants to leave were Mathews and Clarke in 1953 two whole years of trial after the first order to withdraw.

* *Green Leaf in Drought*, by Isobel Kuhn.

The eighty-five-year-old mission to inland China was at an end. The future was veiled in deep darkness. To many it seemed that the Mission could not survive. Was it, then, a case of "mission completed"—or did God have other plans?

## CHAPTER 22

# COUNTER-ATTACK

THROUGH the years many chroniclers have gloomily prophesied the end of the C.I.M. That end was never nearer than in 1951, and the prophets were busy again. The Enemy had delivered what seemed a death blow. Could the Mission survive? Was it intended to survive, or was its commission limited to inland China? Unlike most missions, the C.I.M. had no other fields to which its members could be transferred. "Freehaven" was for them a dead end. In any case, how could those who were still experiencing the trials of their own Dunkirk raise any enthusiasm over a new D-Day? This was a Red Sea experience, and it is only when faced with the humanly impossible that man is utterly cast on the God of the impossible. Man's extremity is always God's opportunity.

As the worn and battered troops retreated to Hong Kong, the Mission's directors from all over the world converged on the small town of Kalorama on the slopes of Mount Dandenong in Australia. The Acting China Director left Shanghai to join them. The home where the seven directors met from April 10th to 17th became the audience chamber where God Himself received them and revealed to them some of the things He was about to do. When they met, about half the number were dubious about attempting to perpetuate the Mission's work. The problems were altogether too vast. The Mission leadership had probably never been confronted by a higher wall of impossibility. But as the men met, they were encouraged by letters and cables from all over the world. During the Conference news reached them that the total evacuation of all missionaries from China had become imperative. As they waited on God it became evident that it was not His will that this battle-hardened and experienced missionary force should now be disbanded. No!, the Mission would remain in existence. Its first duty would be to mobilise prayer for China while cherishing the hope of an eventual return. The younger workers recruited in 1948 and 1949 and other future volunteers, would certainly find opportunities among the millions of "overseas Chinese" in South-east Asia and in the home countries. Senior workers would be needed to lead them. If there were Chinese anywhere not being reached by any other agency it would be a serious dereliction of duty not to take them the Gospel. The directors therefore decided to appoint teams to survey Thailand, Malaya, Indonesia and the Philippines in order to discover the extent of the need. While giving priority to the Chinese, they recognised the possibility of some linguistically-trained tribal workers going to the Bible-less tribes in Thailand and in the Philippines. Japan, however, was in a different category: there were few Chinese there and certainly no tribes. The meeting was most undecided whether the Mission was justified in seeking an entrance into Japan. In the middle of the discussion, there was a break for tea and an opportunity to read the mail which had just arrived.

As the meeting reassembled, there was a smile on Bishop Houghton's face. Calling the meeting to order, he said: "Brethren, I have here a letter which I have just received from the General Director of the Sudan Interior Mission which I would like to read to you:

"Dear Bishop Houghton: My Mission has for some time been considering the possibility of extending our work to Japan where we know the need to be very great. A friend has even given us a cheque for $1,000 to start the project. But our Council is not in favour of such a development. Knowing your present situation and your proximity to Japan, I wonder if you are by any chance contemplating opening work there. If God so guides you I will be happy to hand over this sum of $1,000 to be used for the purpose the donor intended. Yours sincerely . . ."

The smile spread to everyone present. But there was further confirmation to come. Bishop Houghton had also received a second letter by the same post with a cheque for £500 enclosed, a part of which was for a survey of the needs of Japan! The discussion concluded. They agreed to send a team to Japan also to explore the possibilities of commencing work there.

The birds singing in the blue gum-trees outside the Kalorama Council chamber seemed to re-echo the new song of faith and joy that welled up in the hearts of the seven men as they worded a telegram to all the home countries and to Hong Kong: "Lengthen cords, strengthen stakes. While emphasising prayer for China conference unanimously convinced Mission should explore unmet need preparatory to entering new fields from Thailand to Japan. Haggai two five.* Houghton." The passion for the impossible had not died.

John Sinton, the Deputy China Director, returned immediately to Hong Kong, which became the temporary headquarters of the Mission. It fell to him to invite a number of men to form the survey teams and to meet the missionaries as they emerged from China to discuss with them their future.

The surveys revealed first of all the presence of 10 million Chinese in south-east Asia and even some Chinese communities in Japan. Many invitations to commence work among them in Singapore, Malaya, Borneo, Manila, Tokyo and Bangkok were received. But as the survey teams consulted with the mission leaders in the countries concerned, a new pattern of need among the non-Chinese nationals of these countries appeared—a need which existing mission agencies admittedly could not meet. In close consultation, therefore, with these other missions and with their warm approval, the Mission began to regard the following fields as especially their own: the tribal area of north Thailand, the thirteen totally unevangelised provinces in the Chao Phya basin of central Thailand, the Muslims of south Thailand, the northern island of Hokkaido in

* "My Spirit remaineth among you: fear ye not."

Japan and the tribes of the island of Mindoro in the Philippines. The stories of the long and exciting journeys of the survey teams in these strange and different fields would fill a book. The two who travelled in the lovely equatorial islands of Indonesia were acutely aware that these islands had in 1854 moved Hudson Taylor to write from the *Dumfries* on his first voyage to China, "Oh, what work for the missionary! Island after island, many almost unknown, some densely populated, but no Light, no Jesus, no hope full of bliss! My heart yearns over them. Can it be that Christian men and women will stay comfortably at home and leave these souls to perish? Can it be that faith has no longer power to constrain to sacrifice for His sake who gave His life for the world's redemption? Shall we think ourselves free from responsibility to obey the plain command 'Go ye into all the world and preach the Gospel to every creature?' Oh that I could get to them! Oh that I had a thousand tongues to proclaim in every land the riches of God's grace! Lord, raise up labourers, and thrust them forth into Thy harvest." That prayer was initially answered in the sending of Dutch and German missionaries but in 1951 the answer began to come through the members of his own mission. Members of the C.I.M., instead of preaching in the one common language of China, would soon be preaching the Gospel throughout east Asia, in three additional Chinese dialects, six new national languages and a dozen or more tribal tongues.

As the survey teams made their way back to Hong Kong crowds of campers at "Freehaven" eagerly awaited their reports. General relief was felt that God still had a work for the Mission to do. But men and women who had once had a clear call to work in China did not find it easy to discern a new call to work in some other field. Unfamiliar languages would have to be learned and they would need to adapt to strange cultures and climatic conditions. Which need should each try to meet? What type of work offered the right scope? Which of half a dozen possible countries presented the greatest personal challenge? Many hours of prayer and thought were spent in the quiet beauty spots of Hong Kong before the answer to these questions was given. By the end of 1951, while the remnants were still leaving China, fifty-three C.I.M. missionaries were actually in the new fields, and thirty-two at the temporary headquarters in Hong Kong. It was as though God had brought the Mission very low, even down to death, in order to renew its life by resurrection, and multiply its fruitfulness after a fresh blossoming of the old tree. Even the name was new, for "Overseas Missionary Fellowship" was the chosen name by which the C.I.M. became known throughout east Asia. In financial ways, God confirmed the far-reaching decisions taken, for His gifts to the Mission in 1951 amounted to £330,749—enough to cover all the heavy added expenses of survey journeys, directors' conferences, furlough passages and the entry into new fields. God still moves men's hearts to give in response to prayer alone.

In China, the Church was passing through the furnace of affliction. At a Christian conference held in Peking in April the Accusation Movement was launched and then repeated in every church throughout China. Christians were expected to accuse one another; church members accused their pastors; Chinese accused missionaries; the poor accused the rich. The movement was supposed to act as a kind of cathartic to rid the system of all traces of imperialist and feudal influences. The Three-Self Reform Movement of the Church of Christ in China was then inaugurated. Christian leaders were given special extra indoctrination above the normal "learning" in which the whole nation shared. It was a case of conform or suffer. Many chose to suffer, while many chose to conform. Individuals might and did fall but the Church lived on. Many missionaries endured suffering and imprisonment, but they could at least hope for eventual freedom outside China. For Chinese Christians there was no release. Ten years of increasing pressures and subtle inducements finally brought the Church into complete subjection to the Communist Party and deprived it of true freedom. Hundreds of faithful and uncompromising Christians remained in prison, while others were banished to work in labour camps in China's "Siberia". Yet above the storm we hear the irrefutable promise of the Church's Risen and Exalted Head, "I will build My Church and the gates of Hell shall not prevail against it."

From Peking in 1954 there emerged the following anonymous message written on a scrap of thin paper—the testimony of the Chinese Church to the Church throughout the world: "True faith in God does not imply that we anticipate an easy future or believe that God will intervene to crown our righteous cause with an early victory. Faith is not confidence in God's willingness to serve those who seek His support. Faith is surrender to the will of God, even though that will include the dark night of Gethsemane or the anguish of Calvary. Faith is serene trust in God's ability to use all human forces and passions for the fulfilment of His eternal purpose. It is a divinely inspired conviction that God's plans cannot be frustrated, that even the wrath of mankind can be made to praise Him. The man of faith reads both his Bible and the book of history. He beholds there the eternal unity of God's message and God's method. He sees clearly the guiding hand of God in all the movements of the centuries and the changing fortunes of individuals and nations. Yes, the Lord God Omnipotent reigneth. He is still Lord of His own creation. There have been many dark nights in the world's history, but the Sun of Righteousness has always risen to gild again the Western hills with the entrancing dawn of a new day . . . The God who is the same yesterday and today and for ever still controls His own universe. God's tomorrows will be brighter than today."

Professor Joseph Needham of Cambridge University, and an expert on China has written: "Four times in history was China offered the possibility of adopting organised Christianity. But the Mission always failed. And the fact must be faced by Westerners that the Christian religion in its organised forms has been decisively rejected by Chinese culture." As far as "organised Christianity" is concerned, Needham may be right. The Chinese Christians firmly rejected much that was merely Western. But it is emphatically not true that the Chinese people as a whole have rejected

Christ. "God's tomorrows will be brighter than today".

The C.I.M. can never forget the Church in China, a large section of which owes its origin to the eighty-five years' work of its missionaries. While the Mission continues to witness to the other lands of east Asia, it can never relinquish the hope of a return to the Chinese mainland to share with the Church her unfinished task of evangelism.

## CHAPTER 23

# READY SANDALS

AN Indian Christian lad was studying the journeys of the Apostle Paul. "Paul had ready sandals," he said suddenly, thinking of the Apostle's words, "having your feet shod with the preparation of the Gospel of peace". Overhearing the boy's expression, another whispered, "The Lord give us all ready sandals! Christ has so many cool and decorous followers. We don't want to add to their number!"

There were many with ready sandals to run to the overseas Chinese of east Asia. But the pathway was rough. Suspicion and hostility often greeted them. The welcome in Borneo was cool. In Malaya, where Communist terrorists struggled for victory in the jungle, physical danger was never far distant. The refugee needs in Hong Kong were overwhelming. The wealthy and lukewarm churches of the Philippines contrasted sharply with the zeal and comparative poverty of those in China. But O.M.F. missionaries moved in—to a Chinese high school in Manila, to Chinese students in Cebu, to a Bible School in Singapore and to small Chinese churches in west Borneo. A task force of seventy kept the flag flying. The forty-niners who so dramatically reached Chungking as the Communist armies were taking over formed its nucleus. The bold decision was now well justified.

In November 1951 the spotlight moved from Australia to England, from Kalorama to Bournemouth, where twenty-five Mission leaders met to face the implications and problems of the transition from China to new fields of operation. The promises of God remained the only guarantees for pressing forward into the unknown in obedience to the revealed purpose of God. The gathering thoroughly re-examined the Mission's policies and honestly pondered its past failures and mistakes. In the light of recent experiences in China and the changed world situation bold changes of tactics were accepted as inevitable. All agreed that Christian literature must have a high priority in the future programme. The goal of strong indigenous local churches would be kept clearly in view. But there would be no modification at all in the well-tried financial policy of the Mission. Prayer alone would continue to be the Mission's sole resource. As the present Treasurer, Fred Keeble has said, "The currency in which we deal is the promises of God. The Mission is backed 100 per cent by solid bullion, a currency which cannot be debased; for God has said, 'The silver is mine and the gold is mine.'"

A new era in the Mission's long and chequered history was commencing and the man chosen to lead the new outreach was J. Oswald Sanders, an Australian solicitor, with many years experience in Christian administration in Australia, and several as Australasian Home Director of the C.I.M. The headquarters of the Mission was moved from Hong Kong to Singapore, another over-crowded city where property was "impossible to obtain". But within a week or two a suitable building in Chancery Lane was found and bought at just half the price originally asked. The Mission was set to go. In 1952, 130 reinforcements arrived in Singapore to augment the small task force. The work expanded rapidly and by the end of 1953 there were 370 missionaries on the field. The cost of living in east Asia was very high, but a steady rise in the Mission's income covered the increasing costs of the work. In 1954 the headquarters staff moved to a splendid new property in Cluny Road, opposite the beautiful Botanical Gardens, and Chancery Lane became the Language Centre. After four years work, there were small bridgeheads in sixty new places in east Asia. Fruitful evangelism was in full swing and embryo churches were emerging. Eighteen doctors were active in clinic, leprosy and hospital work and the first phase of the Manorom Hospital project was operative. O.M.F. missionaries were on loan to four theological colleges.

Seventy-three new workers reached Singapore in 1955 bringing the total field membership up to 552.

. . .

In accordance with the Bournemouth decision, literature work was given high priority. The Mission had gone into the literature business for the first time after the war in 1948, when a publications department was started by Ken and Vera Price in Shanghai. Two years later a representative meeting of Christian publishers discovered that, in a country of over 500 million people and 1 million Protestant Christians, only twelve Christian books had a circulation of 2,000 and less than six a circulation of 5,000. This was in spite of large publishing houses like the Christian Literature Society and several denominational publishers. Their shelves were bulging with books nobody wanted to read. The subject matter was not vital, the translations of foreign books were often poor and the standpoint of the majority was that of a liberal theology. Moreover, the presentation was unattractive. But the same meeting also noted that two recent books were an exception to the rule: *Hudson Taylor* (C.I.M.) achieved a circulation of 7,000 and *Questions of Faith* (C.I.V.F.) of 20,000 in the first year of their publication! There *was* a market for the right books.

The new agency's first aim was to publish attractive evangelistic leaflets. A mass distribution of those leaflets was organised at a National Sports Meeting in Kiang-wan. Letters at once began to pour in from service men, hospital patients, students and prisoners who had read the leaflets. Two keen Christians in a Nanking jail, falsely incriminated in a notorious case of corruption, bore a clear witness and were allowed to distribute C.I.M. leaflets to the prisoners right up to the time of their execution. The Press quoted freely from their last letters which breathed faith and hope in a glorious resurrection. The Prices moved to Hong Kong in December 1948 to set up the Christian Witness Press and an emergency treasurer's department. Those left in

Shanghai pressed forward with a new hymn book for the Chinese Church, Bible study books and major translations, all of which have had extensive sales. Small libraries were issued to pastors all over China in anticipation of a coming dearth of Christian literature.

The Christian Witness Press made spectacular progress in Hong Kong and was soon publishing in ten languages. 1956 saw the launching of the colourful Chinese language magazine *Dengta* (Lighthouse) which achieved immediate popularity.

. . . .

The witness to overseas Chinese was extending in other ways. Invitations reached the Mission from Chinese churches in Java. Opportunities among students, the armed forces and leprosy sufferers in Taiwan (Formosa) were eagerly seized. Even in Tokyo Chinese Christians welcomed O.M.F. help. But the vision was widening. At Kalorama the concern expressed had been primarily for the 10 million Chinese in east Asia. Now the needs of other nationals were becoming increasingly clamant. A steady stream of missionaries was reaching the central provinces of Thailand to evangelise the Buddhists there. Buddhist monks and a popular actor were among the early converts. Thus the church was planted for the first time in the fertile rice plains of the Chao Phya river. George Harris, the veteran Islamic expert, went in search of the Muslim Malays of south Thailand and medical and evangelistic work began among them. In Indonesia, the Javanese churches invited O.M.F. aid in evangelising the receptive Muslims of east and central Java where conversions were occurring in large numbers and new churches were springing up. The emptiness of the Roman Catholic faith for the people of the Philippines was an invitation to preach the Gospel of free grace to them, and new churches were formed in Batangas and Mindoro. The people of Japan's northern island of Hokkaido were no more responsive than other Japanese, but the Gospel was faithfully preached among the

fisherfolk, farmers and miners. Tent campaigns attracted
large crowds in the summer months.

.    .    .

The C.I.M. interest in the evangelisation of aboriginal
tribespeople goes back before the beginning of the
century. Among the first missionaries to leave China in
1950 were some with long experience in Yunnan.
Sections of the Lisu tribe were known to be scattered
over the hills of north Thailand and Orville Carlson
went in search of them. Quite by accident he and his
companion happened to pass through a village which
turned out to belong to the Yao tribe. The headman
actually spoke Chinese with a Shantung accent, for the
tribe claims to have come originally from that part of
China. It was therefore possible to communicate with
him, in spite of his dulled senses from opium smoking.
Seeing that Chinese smugglers encourage the cultivation of opium in these hills and offer good prices for the
crops, it is not surprising that opium addiction is at a
very high level. "Old Six", the headman, listened to the
first preaching of the Gospel with apathy and appeared
to the missionaries to be a very unlikely potential convert. But as further visits were paid interest grew. "Old
Six" remembered a dream he had had years ago over in
Laos and the coming of the Gospel messengers seemed to
be a fulfilment. The time came when he invited missionaries to stay in his roomy but dingy mountain shack to
teach him more. When he wanted to believe, the elders
of the village actually went to a neighbouring hill-top to
consult the spirits. "Old Six" then went into the nearest
city to break off his opium at the Presbyterian hospital.
His wife also became a believer. They then built a
simple chapel on the hillside and began to hold regular
services. Eric Cox and his family moved into the village
to live in a shack specially constructed for them. But no
one dared to take the step of baptism until "Old Six"
was willing to be the first. That day came at last and the
first Yao church in Thailand came into being. The Yao
tribe—which may number 3 million—is widely scattered

180

over China, Laos, Vietnam and north Thailand. As the missionaries translated and taught the Scriptures the Gospel obtained an even stronger hold on the people of Maesalong. They themselves became missionaries and other villages along the mountain ridge turned from the spirits to the Living God. Opium-growing was abandoned and other legitimate means of livelihood prospered. "Brother Six", the more affectionate name by which missionaries now know the headman, developed strong powers of spiritual leadership and an evangelistic concern and gift. The Yao church is growing fast.

Strangely enough the Lisu, so responsive in Yunnan, are proving singularly unresponsive in Thailand and are bound to their demon worship. Lilian Hamer, the beloved servant of the Lisu, was actually murdered on a mountain trail by one of them. The ardently Buddhist Shan people, after a glimmer of response, put up the shutters to keep out the Light. The Lahu and the Pwo Karen have been hearing the Gospel for ten years but as yet there is little result, although the first conversions have been reported. The Akha have been the strongest challenge to faith and patience. But two Christian Akha from Burma have been courageous missionaries to their own people and a break has taken place: missionaries are now free to live in a Christian village with a small group of Christian Akha. The Blue and the White Meo (Miao) have yielded precious fruits and several men of God are emerging. A second servant of the tribes, Roy Orpin, fell to the guns of murderers while setting up home for his bride among the White Meo. Yet single women missionaries and one or two married couples carry on in the hope and confidence that God is building His Church among the long neglected tribes of north Thailand. There are no easy or quick victories. Isobel Kuhn, the skilful recorder of earlier triumphs among the tribes in China, who with her husband led the first steep ascent to the tribes of Thailand, was the first casualty in the work. She lived long enough to give the world her finest and most widely-read books, including her own best-selling auto-biography *By Searching*.

The challenge of the unreached tribes in Laos came to the Mission in 1956 and the first advance parties crossed the Mekong River from Thailand the following year. The work made a very promising start, but the civil war forced the missionaries back from their advance bases in the tribal areas to the valley of the Mekong where they are co-operating closely with the Swiss Mission Évangelique in work among the Lao. Limited touch with the tribes is maintained in some areas.

The seven tribes in the mountainous island of Mindoro in the Philippines, became the sole responsibility of the O.M.F. There, under the leadership of Jim Broomhall, the results have been much more encouraging. The animism of the Philippines seems to be less sinister and enslaving than that of Laos or Thailand. Hundreds of conversions have occurred and scores of churches have been established. But the work in the Philippines has also suffered the irreparable loss of five workers as the result of accident, death by natural causes or disablement through polio. Several O.M.F. missionaries have a share in the very great opportunity among the tribes in Taiwan. In Thailand, Laos and the Philippines, Bible translation in a dozen tribal tongues is being given high priority.

Thus the work in east Asia, with its 300 million people, grew rapidly. Eighty of the first 130 centres were in virgin areas. When the available workers proved to be quite insufficient, the General Director in 1956 issued an appeal for prayer for 184 new workers. In response, ninety-four reached Singapore in 1957 and sixty-eight the following year. And when the income in 1958 reached the record total of £423,038, there was much cause for praise to God.

But the Mission had taken on many difficult tasks. New languages had to be learned and many obstacles overcome. Compared with China, the results were disappointing. Converts were scarce and few of them were effective witnesses to their own people. The opposition was formidable. It is not surprising that within the Mission there was a growing desire for revival. "Oh

for the flash and the flame of the Spirit among us" was
how the feelings of all were expressed at the 1958 meeting
of the Overseas Council. And this prayer wish was to be
fulfilled.

## CHAPTER 24

# TOWARDS THE MARK

As the C.I.M. moved towards the end of its century of service, it bore none of the marks of old age. The Mission has in fact been entirely rejuvenated. Just over 500 men and women have joined the Mission since 1951. Fifty-eight per cent of the present membership of about 850 have therefore had less than ten years service and are under the age of forty. There is youth and vigour and vision. Like the Apostle Paul, the Mission is still in the race, straining towards the finishing tape. It is not forgetful of the past, but past failures or successes will not be permitted to hold it back from future victories. "I press towards the mark for the prize of the high calling of God in Christ Jesus" is still the spirit of the Mission.

But, looking back, what is the secret of the perennial vigour of the C.I.M.? First of all, it lies in the exercise of a living faith in God, an individual day-by-day trust on the part of each member as well as a corporate faith for material and spiritual supplies. This is the *motive power* behind the work. A total of £1,000,000 was donated during the first forty years of the Mission's history, a further £4,000,000 in the next thirty years, and in the last thirty years the surprising total of £7,000,000. All has been given solely in answer to prayer which is, to say the least, impressive. Secondly, the *message* of the Mission has remained unchanged over the years. The Gospel which the founder believed and proclaimed is being offered unaltered to a very changed world today. Nothing has happened in the realm of Biblical scholarship to shake the Mission's faith in the authority of Holy Scripture. No progress of human society has lessened the need for the identical message preached by the Apostle

Paul in the corrupt society of Rome. Human nature, whether in the West or in the East, has not changed and no impoverished message, however garnished by philanthropic trappings, can adequately meet the need of man in his present moral and social dilemma. The C.I.M. unashamedly preaches the unexpurgated Gospel of Christ and Him crucified. Nothing else can solve the human problem. Finally, the *methods* which have been used in planting autonomous local churches throughout China and east Asia, being Biblical, have received the seal of God's approval. In China and more recently in the wider sphere of east Asia, the establishing of national churches, healthily independent of Western control and support, but in warm fellowship with all churches sharing the same faith, has been the strategic objective of every Mission activity. The strategy has determined the methods and the tactics to be adopted at every stage. In China the results were not in the form of a large, centrally-controlled organisation or denomination, but in the largest single affiliation of communicant Christians in China, gathered into thousands of local churches. It is impossible to estimate the powerful influence throughout China of these Christian communities, and of the presence of tens of thousands of redeemed, transformed and Christ-like lives in every strata of Chinese society.

Working in the wider sphere of east Asia, the strategic objectives remain the same but a new and critical situation has demanded an increased measure of specialisation.

.    .    .

Literature production was high on the list of Mission priorities. The importance of this work cannot be exaggerated. The Christian Witness Press at Hong Kong is the heart of the Mission's literature outreach. There commentaries, biographies, apologetic literature, Bible Study aids, Scripture Gift Mission publications, Scripture Union notes and millions of evangelistic leaflets for children and the wider public pour off the presses. The

*Lighthouse* magazine has successfully broken into a highly competitive market and now has a world-wide distribution among Chinese in over sixty countries. But the increase of literature distribution in the Philippines was so phenomenal that it was necessary to establish the separate Overseas Missionary Fellowship Publishers in Manila, which is now producing its own literature as well as importing material from Hong Kong. The turnover seems to double each year with a particularly heavy demand for evangelical literature in the English language. There is a well-patronised bookshop in downtown Manila, another in Baguio, and several bookshops on the islands of Mindoro and Mindanao: others are projected. The Literature agency of the Indonesian National Church very courteously sponsored the entry of O.M.F. workers for co-operation with them. Their numerous bookshops distribute vast quantities of books and tracts produced and printed by the O.M.F. in Djakarta. Supply seldom keeps up with demand. In 1964 a consignment of 810 reams of paper was imported from Japan to help meet the paper shortage in that country. In 1959 a bookshop was set up in Tainan, one of the main cities of Taiwan (Formosa), which is helping to meet the demand among the 11 million Chinese on the island. O.M.F. missionaries are also in charge of the Evangel Press Bookshop in Kuala Lumpur. Bangkok, the capital of Thailand, is not the easiest place to pursue a literature programme. There are great problems with production, printing and distribution. Thai writers are few, printing is complicated and the demand not yet great. Moreover, the Thai Church has so far little appetite for Christian literature. But a good start has been made. The newest literature outreach is in Japan, where there is no question about an appetite for reading. The Japanese are voracious readers, 99 per cent of the population being literate. The first bookshop in the university town of Hirosaki was so successful that another was opened in Hakodate, the main port of Hokkaido. In all these centres the biography of James Hudson Taylor is a popular item. Realising that the bottleneck in literature production is the lack of national writers, the

Mission is providing trained journalists to hold schools of writing and journalism in several countries and is conducting competitions to encourage new writers.

.    .    .

The students of Asia immediately claimed the attention of those who left China fresh from seeing the great movement of the Spirit in the universities there. O.M.F. missionaries at once became involved in student work in Manila, Singapore, Djakarta, Taiwan (Formosa) and Japan. More recently workers have been appointed in Bangkok. There has been close co-operation with the Fellowship of Evangelical Students and in some cases workers have been loaned to the local national Inter-Varsity Fellowships. There are several million college and many million high school students in east Asia, a field which can be neglected only at great loss. If the churches are to meet the challenge of the new age their future leadership should be provided very largely by the educated new generation.

.    .    .

Medical work is a traditional feature of the Mission's evangelistic programme. The early surveys in south-east Asia suggested that Thailand should have the first claim on medical personnel. The initial clinics in central and south Thailand were succeeded by hospitals which are growing in size and efficiency. Their ministry has been highly effective, both in the evangelistic outreach and in the training of young converts on the staff to become mature Christian leaders of the churches. Leprosy work in central and south Thailand is an urgent need. In central Thailand the work of the leprosy clinics is well advanced, and a new leprosy wing has been added to the Manorom Hospital. The churches composed of leprosy sufferers are the most encouraging feature of the work in the central provinces. In north Malaya, the Mission accepted responsibility for some of the former Red Cross clinics which have provided good openings for a doctor and several nurses. The Salvation Army hospital in Turen, Java, was without a doctor and therefore invited Dr. Rupert Clarke and his wife, who have conducted a fruitful ministry there: the hospital is in an area where the movement of Muslims towards Christianity has been spectacular. A new hospital is planned for Pakanbaru in central Sumatra. In the Philippines the Mission adopted a scheme, with the Government's approval, of providing medical services for the tribal people of Mindoro, but this work has been temporarily suspended for want of a doctor. Finally, doctors were appointed to north Japan, where a clinic has been a useful focus of evangelism in Aomori, and also caters for the needs of the missionaries in this area.

. . .

As the O.M.F. moved into the new fields of east Asia, it was by no means the first Mission there as it had been in inland China. Much fine work and many old-established churches were in existence. But where pioneer work was not required there was wide scope for cooperation with existing churches and institutions belonging to other organisations. National independent churches in Indonesia and Taiwan (Formosa) sponsored O.M.F. missionaries to work with them in a ministry of Bible teaching. A number of theological colleges and Bible Schools invited the O.M.F. to supply teachers. Qualified members of the Mission were seconded to university staffs in Java, Singapore and Taiwan (Formosa). Others accepted invitations to staff the bookrooms of the China Sunday School Union in Hong Kong and Taipeh. One of the first of the '48 recruits to leave China went direct to Manila to join the staff of the Far Eastern Broadcasting Company, where he became one of the Company's electronic experts; he was given the responsibility of transporting a transmitting station from California to Okinawa and reassembling it there to broadcast the Gospel to China. O.M.F. missionaries also co-operate in F.E.B.C. studios, which prepare tape-recorded programmes in several languages for transmission over the stations of the F.E.B.C. Radio work also features prominently in Japan.

.    .    .

So, year by year, since 1951, the work has grown. The Mission is the largest missionary force in Thailand and Malaya. Its missionaries have become proficient in the new languages and are at home in the new cultures. Converts are increasing. Leaders are being trained. The new churches are growing in size and responsibility. In every field the O.M.F. contribution to evangelical co-operation is increasingly appreciated. The hard decision of 1951 has been justified. Instead of serving but one nation, the Fellowship is today ministering to seven. Its outreach in the sphere of literature is among the most significant in east Asia. From the ashes of the 1951 conflagration a new phoenix has arisen. The impossible has become a glorious reality. The future, despite the political clouds, is full of hope, because bright with the promises of God with whom nothing is impossible.

# BIBLIOGRAPHY

*Hudson Taylor*, Vols. I & II, Dr. & Mrs. Howard Taylor. C.I.M.

*The Man Who Believed God*, by Marshall Broomhall. C.I.M.

*Hudson Taylor and Maria*, by John Pollock. Hodder and Stoughton

*These Forty Years*, by F. Howard Taylor. Pepper Publishing Co.

*The Story of the China Inland Mission*, by Geraldine Guinness.

*The Jubilee Story of the China Inland Mission*, by Marshall Broomhall. C.I.M.

*Borden of Yale*, by Mrs. Howard Taylor. C.I.M.

*Green Leaf in Drought*, by Isobel Kuhn. C.I.M.

*Pastor Hsi*, by Mrs. Howard Taylor. C.I.M.

*Behind the Ranges*, by Mrs. Howard Taylor. C.I.M.

*Strong Man's Prey*, by Jim Broomhall. C.I.M.

*China and the Cross*, by Carey-Elwes. Longmans

*History of Christianity in China*, by K. S. Latourette

*Among the tribes in South-West China*, by Samuel Clarke. Marshall, Morgan and Scott